UNSTOPPABLE!

The CHICAGO BLACKHAWKS' Dominant 2013 Championship Season

AP Images

This book is available in quantity at special discounts for your group or organization.
For further information, contact:

Triumph Books LLC
814 North Franklin Street
Chicago, Illinois 60610
Phone: (312) 337-0747
www.triumphbooks.com

Printed in U.S.A.
ISBN: 978-1-60078-891-8

Daily Herald
Douglas K. Ray: Chairman, Publisher and CEO
Colin M. O'Donnell: Senior Vice President/Director of Content
John Lampinen: Senior Vice President/Editor
Jim Baumann: Assistant Vice President/Managing Editor
Tom Quinlan: Sports Editor
Contributors: Tim Sassone, Barry Rozner, Mike Spellman, Travis Siebrass, Teresa Schmedding, Joe Aguilar, Tim Broderick, Eileen Brown, Diane Dungey, Don Friske, John Deitz, Marty Stengle, Aaron Gabriel, Jeff Knox, and Chris Hankins

Content packaged by Mojo Media, Inc.
Joe Funk: Editor
Jason Hinman: Creative Director

Front and back cover photos by Getty Images.

AP Images

CONTENTS

INTRODUCTION

BLACKHAWKS' UNFORGETTABLE ROAD TO THE STANLEY CUP

By Tim Sassone

Talk about a storybook season.

The Blackhawks had one in 2013.

The season didn't start until mid-January in Los Angeles because of the lockout, and 24 games into the schedule the Hawks still hadn't suffered a loss in regulation, establishing an NHL record for best start by going 21-0-3.

The Hawks didn't lose more than two games in a row in the regular season, finishing with 11 wins in their last 15 games.

They capped the memorable season by disposing of Minnesota in the first round of the playoffs, rallying from a 3-1 deficit against Detroit in an epic seven-game series in the second round that wasn't decided until overtime in Game 7, then knocking off defending champion Los Angeles in the Western Conference finals and coming up strong against Boston in Game 6 with two third-period goals in the final minutes of the Stanley Cup Final.

The first game of the Final against the Bruins took three overtimes to decide, and the deciding game appeared headed to overtime until Bryan Bickell and Dave Bolland each found the net 17 seconds apart with the game-winner coming at 19:01 in the third period.

It was the Hawks' second Stanley Cup in four years, but there were only eight players who played on both teams for coach Joel Quenneville — Jonathan Toews, Patrick Sharp, Marian Hossa, Patrick Kane, Duncan Keith, Brent Seabrook, Dave Bolland and Niklas Hjalmarsson.

Hawks general manager Stan Bowman, who didn't get enough credit for the first Stanley Cup win in his rookie year as GM, rebuilt more than half the club after salary cap problems forced him to tear the 2010 champs apart.

"When we look back, we had to change the whole makeup of our team, basically half the team, after winning," Quenneville said. "It was kind of a new team for a couple years there. I thought we progressed over the course of a few years there.

"At the same time — the challenges this year — we got off to an amazing start. I thought we faced as much adversity as you can face being down 3-1 against Detroit."

Bowman kept the core mostly intact, re-signing Toews, Kane, Sharp, Keith, Seabrook

Blackhawks captain Jonathan Toews hoists the Stanley Cup after Chicago's thrilling 3-2 victory in Game 6 to clinch the Stanley Cup. (AP Images)

STANLEY CUP
CHAMPIONS
FINAL

and Hjalmarsson to contract extensions.

To replace those players they couldn't afford to keep, the Hawks developed their own prospects in goalie Corey Crawford, left wing Bryan Bickell, right wing Andrew Shaw, left wing Brandon Saad and center Marcus Kruger.

Bowman traded for defensemen Nick Leddy and Johnny Oduya, left wings Michael Frolik and Viktor Stalberg, and center Michal Handzus. He signed right wing Jamal Mayers, goalie Ray Emery, left wing Daniel Carcillo, defensemen Michal Rozsival and Sheldon Brookbank and left wing Brandon Bollig as free agents.

And, poof, it all came together.

"It seemed like we had a different guy step up every night," Toews said.

The comparisons with the 2010 team are only natural to discuss.

"Certainly the core group has matured to a nice level over the last four years," Quenneville said. "We've got some young guys this year who made a big impact on our team, have grown throughout the year and in the playoffs as well.

"You look back to the group in 2010 ... maybe the makeup is a little bit different to the team, but certainly the objective, the demographics are comparable. We had a young team, we still feel we have a young team today."

Bowman, just as he didn't seek the credit in 2010, was quick to deflect the praise coming his way now.

"I try to point out that it really is sort of a team effort," Bowman said. "It's not just one man. It wasn't one man back then. It's not one man now.

"I look at some of the success we've had personnel-wise and you have to look at our amateur scouting staff. They've done a great job. We've had a couple young players, Andrew Shaw, Brandon Saad — they've come in at a young age, made a big contribution. Once we get the players, we turn them over to the coaches, they have to find a way to utilize them, make them better players. They've done that."

Keeping the Hawks at the top of the league is Bowman's goal.

"I think everyone that has success wants to sustain that over a period of time," Bowman said. "It's a challenge to do it. Obviously, there are a lot of factors that come into play in the salary cap world.

"I think it can be done, clearly. You have to have some continuity to your team. Obviously, there are some changes from year to year. We want to keep these guys together as much as we can and to keep developing as a group. I certainly hope it's a trend that we continue. I think the fans in Chicago have come to love the team. They're supporting us like never before. We want to keep that going."

Keith would like to see this team stick around a little longer than the 2010 champs.

"I think we've all matured over the last few years," Keith said. "We've learned a lot, especially losing back-to-back years in the first round. It's basically been the same team that's done that. We've grown together a lot the last three years as a group."

Some GMs might have blown the team up after two straight first-round exits in the playoffs, but not Bowman.

"We did a lot of good things the last couple seasons," Bowman said. "You have to have confidence that you're close to having success in the playoffs. I think we knew we had a very good team. We didn't need to make sweeping changes.

"I think there's something to be said for consistency. We've had a lot of these guys together for a long time. Certainly Joel has done a great job. He understands how to coach the team. There are a lot of little nuances that the media doesn't see or the fans may not pick up on. When you add it all up, that's why we felt confident coming into the year that we had the group that could have success."

Kane said the core players from 2010 are better players now.

"I think a lot of us that were here in 2010, we consider we're better players now," Kane said. "I myself feel that I'm a well-rounded player, got a lot better defensively and without the puck as time has gone on. I feel like I'm more focused about hockey now." ■

Blackhawks coach Joel Quenneville celebrates with Dave Bolland following the Blackhawks' thrilling victory in Game 6 of the Stanley Cup Final. (AP Images)

STANLEY CUP FINAL, **GAME 1**

JUNE 12, 2013 • BLACKHAWKS 4, BRUINS 3, (3OT)

MARATHON VICTORY

Long, Long Opening Act Ends in Win for Hawks

By Tim Sassone

Andrew Shaw seemed to be everywhere Wednesday night in Game 1 of the Stanley Cup Finals.

Shaw sure was in the right place at the right time in front of the net in triple overtime, when he deflected a shot by Michal Rozsival past goalie Tuukka Rask to give the Blackhawks a 4-3 win over Boston.

The clock in the United Center had just struck midnight when Shaw ended the third-longest game in team history at 12:08 of the third OT. The longest game in team history took place in 1931, when Cy Wentworth scored at 13:50 of the third OT to beat Montreal.

Rozsival's shot was tipped first by Dave Bolland before Shaw got a piece of it.

The Hawks got third-period goals from Bolland and Johnny Oduya to force overtime.

Hawks goalie Corey Crawford was sensational with 51 saves, coming up big on two Bruins power plays in overtime. Both penalties were for the Hawks having too many men on the ice.

"It's what we've come to expect from him," Patrick Sharp said.

"Crow was great. He kept us in there," Hawks coach Joel Quenneville said. "He made several all-alone plays and saves. He was great. There were a lot of pucks at the net, a lot of bouncing pucks with traffic, and a big penalty kill as well."

Crawford stopped Shawn Thornton on a 2-on-1 in the first overtime and later stood tall on Boston's first power play.

"You just have to stick with it, no matter if you miss or if they come close," Crawford said. "You have to keep going until you win.

The Hawks got another penalty for too many men on the ice at 19:03 of the second overtime and got lucky when Jaromir Jagr deflected a Zdeno Chara shot off the right post.

In the third OT moments before Shaw scored, Kaspars Daugavins had a chance all alone in front only to be pulled down by Oduya just as he was getting ready to pull the trigger on a backhander in a wide-open net.

"I don't really know what happened," Oduya said. "I was trying to put my stick there and try to force him to do something. I got lucky on that play, I think, getting my stick in so he couldn't get the shot off."

The Hawks outshot Boston 39-25 through regulation and scored 2 goals in the last 12 minutes to send the game to overtime.

After Patrice Bergeron scored on a power play at 6:09 to give the Bruins a 3-1 lead, Bolland and Oduya answered with goals less than five minutes apart and the comeback was on.

Bolland got his first of the playoffs at the eight-minute mark on a feed from Shaw after a Torey Krug turnover. Shaw spotted Bolland

Dave Bolland celebrates after scoring the second of the Blackhawks' two goals late in the third period. Bolland's goal proved to be the game-winner. (AP Images)

CCM
FINAL
Reebok
Reebok

streaking down the left side and found him with a sweet pass through traffic.

Oduya got the Hawks their first tie of the night at 12:14, when his shot hit the skate of defenseman Andrew Ference and trickled by Rask.

Boston scored the only goal of the first period at 13:11 when Milan Lucic beat Crawford on a pass from Nathan Horton.

Bruins 6-foot-9, 255-pound defenseman Zdeno Chara played 45:05 and was a guy the Hawks appeared to be ready for. Duncan Keith played more than 48 minutes.

"He's definitely a factor," Quenneville said of Chara. "Not too many guys you're going to go down inside and expect to beat him 1-on-1. We want to make it challenging for him. At the same time, that could be easier said than done. But he does play big minutes. You try to wear him down, work him in his own zone. He's a special defenseman."

Shaw, all of 5-10, 180 pounds, went right at Chara on several occasions.

"He's a competitor" Quenneville said of Shaw. "He does things game in, game out. The bigger the stage, the bigger the challenge; he rises to the occasion. He's a warrior."

Niklas Hjalmarsson went for a hit on David Krejci behind the net and missed. Krejci came away with the puck and fed Horton, whose touch pass to Lucic caught Crawford out of position to make the stop.

Another poor read by Hjalmarsson led to Lucic's second goal 51 seconds into the second period.

The Hawks got a goal from Saad a short time later to make it 2-1. It was Saad's first goal of the playoffs in his 18th game. Saad had 6 of the Hawks' 39 shots through regulation and Marian Hossa 8.

The Hawks had a chance to make it 2-2, but they failed to cash in on 1:17 of a 5-on-3 near the midpoint of the second period.

"It's never easy to lose a game when you're in the third overtime period," Bruins coach Claude Julien said. "I thought that in overtime we got better. We got a little stronger.

"We had some great looks, some great opportunities and just didn't bury them. Eventually somebody is going to score a goal as fatigue sets in." ■

Corey Crawford blocks a shot by Boston Bruins left wing Milan Lucic late in the third period of Game 1. Crawford totaled 51 saves in the win. (John Starks/Daily Herald)

17
Reebok
Reebok

STANLEY CUP FINAL, GAME 2

JUNE 15, 2013 • BRUINS 2, BLACKHAWKS 1 (OT)

OVERTIME AGONY

For Hawks, No Celebrating this Time

By Tim Sassone

For the second time in two games, the Blackhawks and the Bruins needed extra time to decide a winner.

This time it wasn't the Hawks doing the celebrating.

Daniel Paille's goal at 13:48 of the first overtime gave Boston a 2-1 win and evened the Stanley Cup Final at 1-1.

Brandon Bollig, who was playing for the second straight game in the Final for the benched Viktor Stalberg, couldn't handle a rim-around off the boards, and the Bruins pounced on the opportunity.

Tyler Seguin fed Paille between the circles, and he beat Corey Crawford to the glove side off the post.

Paille also assisted on Chris Kelly's goal at 14:58 of the second period that made it 1-1.

Bruins coach Claude Julien put fourth liners Kelly and Paille with third liner Seguin together after the first period, and it paid off with magic.

"We didn't have much going, and I thought that line would give us something, and they responded well," Julien said. "They got both goals tonight. It was a hunch from the coach.

"You look at last game when they won and their heroes were guys from the third and fourth lines. That's what you get in the playoffs. Top lines are playing head to head and against top defensemen, so it's not always that easy to score."

The Hawks regretted coming out of the first period ahead only 1-0 despite dominating the play.

"The first period was a period that we were really disappointed with," Julien said. "From the second period on we seemed to slowly get better and better. The further the games went on, the better we got. Obviously, when you come into this building you're hoping for a split.

"That first period was a hard period to coach and to watch. They were skating and we weren't."

The Hawks attempted 30 shots to Boston's 5 with 19 getting to the net.

The Hawks got the only goal of the period at 11:22 when Patrick Sharp beat Bruins goalie Tuukka Rask from the far right side during a scramble.

Unfortunately for the Hawks, that was all they could put behind Rask, and it came back to bite them in the end.

"Maybe we left something out there," Hawks coach Joel Quenneville said. "Had everything right in that first part of the game. Had some good looks, as well. Did what we were looking to do. But, hey, it's a long game. We've got to be better than that.

"I thought we slowed ourselves down. I don't think we got the puck behind them. I think we were in front of them too much and that played into their hands. In the second period, I thought we lost the pace of the game on that end of the rink.

Zdeno Chara, Boston's 6-foot-9, 255-pound defenseman, checks Jonathan Toews into the boards. The Bruins effectively threw their weight around against the Blackhawks in Game 2. (Steve Lundy/Daily Herald)

CHARA
33
19
BAUER
Reebok

"We had the perfect start to the game and then we stopped doing what made us successful. We stood around and they countered."

The Hawks let the Bruins hang around until late in the second period when a turnover by defenseman Nick Leddy led to Kelly's tying goal at 14:58.

"If somebody would watch the first period, I would've said, 'Oh, give them the Cup right now,'" Jaromir Jagr said. "If somebody watched the overtime, they say, 'Oh, it's gonna be a long series.'"

"I don't think we played well enough to win that one in overtime at all," said Hawks defenseman Brent Seabrook. "We came out in the second firing and we have to do a better job of keeping the momentum throughout the game."

The Hawks' power play was a problem once again, going 0-for-3 and looking disorganized and unsure of itself.

Quenneville thought the power play had a few good looks.

"Two good looks on the first one," Quenneville said. "I thought that was our two nice setups. We lost a little momentum on the next one or two."

The outcome might have been different had Jonathan Toews' goal late in the first period been allowed to stand. Replays showed the puck clearly over the goal line, but the referee told Quenneville he was in the process of blowing the whistle.

"He said his intention was to blow the whistle," Quenneville said.

"I thought the whistle was a little quick, but that's the way it is," Toews said.

Quenneville had no problems with the play by Bollig in overtime.

"They got the one shift, around the wall, we didn't get there in time, bang, bang," Quenneville said.

"No one said it was going to be easy," Toews said. "No one said everything was going to go our way. Some moments, you feel pretty darn good, like when we won Game 1 and triple overtime, and tonight it doesn't feel good.

"You've got to find a way to get over it to move to the next time you're going to be on the ice, and not let it affect you." ■

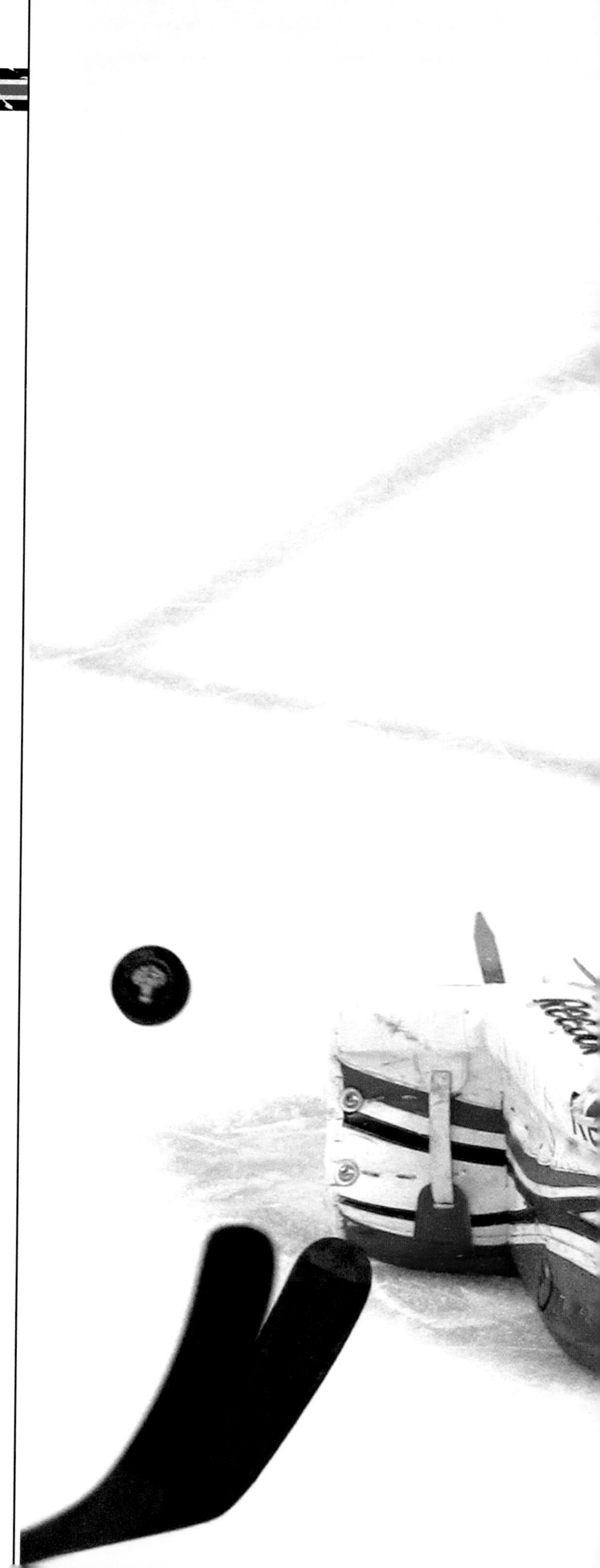

Corey Crawford makes a save during Game 2. Crawford had 26 saves in the loss. (Steve Lundy/Daily Herald)

50
FINAL
CRAWFORD
Reebok
Reebok

STANLEY CUP FINAL, GAME 3

JUNE 17, 2013 • BRUINS 2, BLACKHAWKS 0

BOXED OUT IN BOSTON

Tough Go for Blackhawks without Hossa

By Tim Sassone

The Blackhawks managed to win without Duncan Keith in the last round, but they couldn't beat the Boston Bruins without Marian Hossa.

After trying to take the warm-up, Hossa was a late scratch with an upper-body injury and the Hawks couldn't overcome the loss of their second-best all-around player.

The result was a 2-0 loss to the Bruins at TD Garden in Game 3 of the Stanley Cup Final.

"We're hopeful he'll be ready for the next game," Hawks coach Joel Quenneville said.

The Bruins lead the series 2-1.

"It's something we were prepared for all day that he might not play," captain Jonathan Toews said. "It happens sometimes that you're missing one of your best players and you've got to find a way to play without him."

Patrick Sharp said playing without Hossa was no excuse for the loss.

"We found out after warm-ups that he wasn't going to play," Sharp said. "We've got plenty of guys that can step up. You take a guy like that out of the lineup and it hurts, but it's definitely not the excuse we're going to use.

"We had plenty of chances to make a difference out there, and we didn't."

Bruins coach Claude Julien said he found out Hossa wasn't playing when everyone else did.

"Just found out when I received the game sheet," Julien said. "I was surprised as anybody else. But to be honest with you, there weren't any changes in our game. As I mentioned the other day when I was asked about another player, we don't make our game plan based on an individual.

"I can definitely tell you they lost a pretty important player on their roster, but that doesn't mean we change our game. I think it's important we stick with what we believe in."

Only Corey Crawford's strong play in goal for the Hawks with 33 saves kept it close.

The Hawks now have just 1 goal against Bruins goalie Tuukka Rask on the last two games.

"I don't think (he's in our head)," Toews said. "The last two series there have been times when we had trouble scoring goals. Sometimes it happens. We've just got to be better and work harder for those loose pucks."

While the Hawks flailed again on the power play, going 0-for-3, Boston got a power-play goal in the second period from Patrice Bergeron to make it 2-0, and the game was over.

Again, the Hawks spent most of their time on the perimeter, unable to get inside on the Bruins.

"They box you out," Quenneville said. "They've got big bodies. They block shots. I think we had some chances to get some pucks through the net, but we didn't. Our entries weren't great."

"We maybe took a few too many penalties,

and we didn't create on our power play," Toews said. "As soon as we get one that confidence is going to come.

"We stuck with it for 60 minutes, but we just didn't score enough goals to win. We didn't score any goals. We've got a day to think about it and regroup. I don't think we're discouraged or frustrated at all."

Ben Smith filled in for Hossa, making his first appearance in the playoffs for the Hawks since 2011 when he had 3 goals in the seven-game series against Vancouver. Smith was minus-1 playing with Dave Bolland and Sharp.

Hossa's absence forced Quenneville to radically alter his lines, using Toews with fourth liners Michael Frolik and Marcus Kruger for the first half of the game.

Quenneville was trying to keep Toews away from Bruins defenseman Zdeno Chara, but he may have outsmarted himself as Chara was on the ice for every one of Toews' shifts in the first period.

"It's always good to shake things up a little bit," Toews said. "You might get a little chemistry. Myself, I've been playing against the (David) Krejci line for the most part."

The Hawks were 0-for-2 on the power play in a scoreless first period and almost got scored on twice on the second one with Shawn Thornton off for roughing at 14:15.

Brad Marchand had the puck roll off his stick on a partial breakaway on Boston's best short-handed chance.

Daniel Paille opened the scoring at 2:13 of the second period after Bolland fanned when trying to control the puck. Bergeron's goal came at 14:05 just as a 5-on-3 was expiring.

"It just came down to a couple plays, that's all," Keith said. "We played hard, it was just a couple plays that made the difference."

The Bruins won 71 percent of the faceoffs as Michal Handzus was 0-for-10 and Bolland 1-7. Bergeron was 24-4 for Boston.

"You can talk about that and our power play," Quenneville said. "Those were basically the differentials in the game." ■

Patrice Bergeron, who scored the Bruins' second goal in the second period, maneuvers the puck between Corey Crawford and Johnny Oduya. (AP Images)

STANLEY CUP FINAL, GAME 4

JUNE 19, 2013 • BLACKHAWKS 6, BRUINS 5 (OT)

SERIES-TYING STUNNER

Seabrook's Goal Gives Hawks a Win They Had to Have

By Tim Sassone

In the Blackhawks' previous biggest game of the year, against Detroit in Game 7 of the Western Conference semifinals, it was Brent Seabrook who ended it with a goal in overtime.

In a game Wednesday night that winger Bryan Bickell called the biggest game of some of their lives, it was Seabrook scoring again in overtime at 9:51 to give the Hawks a wild 6-5 road win over Boston in Game 4 of the Stanley Cup Final.

Seabrook beat Bruins goalie Tuukka Rask through a Jonathan Toews screen on a slap shot from the right point to give the Hawks a happy ending in a game in which they lost multiple leads.

"It's one of those things we talked about all year, getting to the net," Seabrook said. "Tazer made a great screen in front, and I just tried to get it on net.

"I just tried to get it past the first guy. I thought all the forwards on the ice did a good job of getting in front and boxing out."

Toews didn't get an assist on the winning goal, but he occupied two defenders in front, including Zdeno Chara.

"I definitely have to give credit to Seabrook for the shot he made," Toews said. "Maybe Rask didn't see it at first. I think I kind of pivoted and maybe let him see it. Obviously it was a little too late.

"(Patrick) Kane's goal came from two guys being in front with traffic. Ugly goals; we don't care. We'll find a way. It's something we need to keep doing."

The win tied the series at 2-2.

"There's definitely a big difference between going back tied and being down 3-1," Hawks goalie Corey Crawford said.

Johnny Boychuk's goal with 7:46 to play sent the game to overtime tied at 5-5 after Patrick Sharp scored on a power play at 11:19.

Sharp's goal put the Hawks ahead for the third time at 5-4.

"It was entertaining hockey and a lot of fun, especially with us winning," Sharp said. "Two good teams. It's easy to say that because we won, but this has been a great series.

"We feel good about going home, best of three with two home games, but I don't think it matters where we play. Boston has been tough to play against in their building and they've been tough in Chicago."

Patrice Bergeron's goal 2:05 into the third period on a shot Crawford probably would like back tied the game 4-4. The Hawks had leads of 1-0, 3-1, 4-2 and 5-4 and couldn't hold off the Bruins.

"They keep coming," Hawks coach Joel Quenneville said. "They're a hardworking team with skill on all their lines. They have a mobile and active defense. They have big shots. Defensively you're always going to get challenged and tested,

Brent Seabrook (front), who would eventually score the crucial game-winning and series-tying goal in overtime, patrols the ice in Game 4. (AP Images)

UMASS LOWELL
2013 CHAMPIONS
COUNT US IN
4:47
BOSTON
BRUINS
STANLEY CUP
CHAMPIONS
1929
BAUER
C
19
OPTIMA
Coors
GEICO

but I thought we did a better job of our offense putting some pressure on their defense."

There were 5 goals scored in the second period alone, 3 by the Hawks.

In a wild second period that couldn't end fast enough for the Hawks, goals by Toews and Patrick Kane a little more than two minutes apart snapped a 1-1 tie.

Both goals were set up by Michal Rozsival point shots.

Quenneville again pushed the right button by reuniting Toews, Kane and Bickell as a line.

Toews got his second goal of the playoffs at 6:33 when he tipped a Rozsival right point shot past Rask.

Kane got his seventh goal of the playoffs at 8:41 when he got a long rebound of a shot by Bickell and backhanded it past Rask.

Rozsival's point shot started the sequence.

Then the goals started coming fast and furious.

The Bruins got a goal from Milan Lucic from in the slot at 14:43 of the second period to make it a 1-goal game again, but Marcus Kruger got that goal right back less than a minutes later at 15:32.

The Bruins dug down deep and pulled within 4-3 at 17:22 on Bergeron's fluky power-play goal.

A shot from straight out by Chara was deflected in front, bounced off the glass behind Crawford, went straight up in the air and dropped in the crease for Bergeron to bang home.

The Hawks got the start Quenneville wanted when Michal Handzus scored short-handed at 6:48 on a 2-on-1 with Brandon Saad. But Saad gave it right back when his turnover allowed the Bruins' Rich Peverley to score on a power play at 14:43 to tie it.

"I don't think anyone expected that before the game," Rask said of the 11 goals scored. "They're a good offensive team. When you give them goals and they get the lead, obviously you have to start opening up, too, and creating some offense. That's what happened."

"I don't think we played our best game tonight for a lot of different reasons," Bruins coach Claude Julien said. "They came out hard and played extremely well. Somehow, again, they had the better of us for the first half of the game until we got ourselves going here a little bit.

"Those are things that happen in the Final where you don't feel like you played well enough to win." ■

Patrick Kane (88) backhands the puck into the net for a goal against Bruins goalie Tuukka Rask in Game 4. Kane's goal gave the Blackhawks a 3-1 second-period lead. (AP Images)

TD GARDEN
1 11:21 2
BOSTON BRUINS
STANLEY CUP CHAMPIONS
1929
BOSTON BRUINS
STANLEY CUP CHAMPIONS
2011
UMASS LOWELL
2013 CHAMPIONS
RASK
40
19
21
Reebok
VAUGHN
VAUGHN
DUNKIN' DONUTS
iRobot

STANLEY CUP FINAL, GAME 5

JUNE 22, 2013 • BLACKHAWKS 3, BRUINS 1

MADNESS ON MADISON

Kane, Rock-Solid Crawford Star on Grandest Stage

By Tim Sassone

The bigger the game, the better Patrick Kane plays.

The guy who scored in overtime in Philadelphia four years ago to give the Blackhawks their first Stanley Cup in 49 years was at it again Saturday night on the game's grandest stage in the Stanley Cup Final in Chicago.

Kane scored 2 goals to back the rock-solid goaltending of Corey Crawford in a 3-1 win over Boston that moved the Hawks within a game of another championship.

The Hawks finished the game without captain Jonathan Toews, who didn't play a shift in the third period because of what Hawks coach Joel Quenneville called an upper body injury.

Toews, who never left the bench for the third period, took two big hits in the head area from Bruins defensemen Johnny Boychuk and Zdeno Chara before leaving.

"We're hopeful he'll be ready next game," Quenneville said. "We'll see how he is (Sunday). I checked on him a couple times; I think he wanted to play."

Both teams ended the game without their best player as Boston's Patrice Bergeron was taken to the hospital for observation after the second period for an undisclosed injury.

Boychuk felt his hit on Toews was legal.

"I came across and read it and hit him," Boychuk said. "I tried to hit him clean and I thought it was. I don't know how he fell, awkwardly or how he fell. I'm going to try and play physical and he's going to drive the net like he's supposed to and I'm going to hit."

Asked if he was concerned about a possible hearing, Boychuk said: "No. I'm pretty sure it was clean."

Toews' teammates were glad just have him on the bench.

"It's always good to have Johnny, if he's not on the ice, just to have him there with the team," defenseman Duncan Keith said.

Kane scored late in the first period and again early in the second to give Crawford all the offense he needed.

Kane got his first goal at 17:27 of the first period on a rebound tuck of a Johnny Oduya point shot.

Kane got his second goal and ninth of the playoffs at 5:15 of the second period on a rebound of a wraparound try by Bryan Bickell, who made a nice power move to the net.

"I think I was in the right spot at the right time tonight on both goals," Kane said. "I thought I had some other chances, too, I could have

Patrick Kane turns toward his teammates to celebrate after scoring one of his two goals in Game 5. (John Starks/Daily Herald)

BAUER
DD
Bauer

scored. But I think playing with Johnny and Bicks, they create a lot of space, and I've been taking advantage of the space they do make.

"I think everyone wants to be that guy in big-time games, and I've been lucky enough in a couple to step up."

There isn't a player in the NHL who looks more comfortable with the puck on his stick than Kane.

"He's dynamic with the puck," Keith said. "There's no guy I'd rather have going down the ice with the puck and following the play than him."

That's 3 goals in the last two games for Kane.

"He's very good at kind of finding those quiet areas and sliding into the right spot," Bruins coach Claude Julien said. "That's why he's a good player and scores a lot of goals. We just maybe have to have a little bit more awareness around our net because both goals were scored the same way."

The Hawks claimed they aren't even thinking they are 1 win away from another Stanley Cup.

"We know the situation, but we're not going to get ahead of ourselves," Keith said. "There's a lot of sacrifice to be made yet. We're excited about this opportunity."

"I'm sure guys are going to think about it, yeah," Brent Seabrook said. "Absolutely. It's the Stanley Cup. But we've got to try to put that in the back of our mind and we know we have a job to do and we've got to get a big start and be ready to play on Monday."

The Bruins came fast and furious at the Hawks in the third period, getting a goal from Chara at 3:40 on a rocket past Crawford from the left faceoff dot.

The game wasn't decided until Dave Bolland scored into an empty net with 14 seconds remaining.

Boston won Games 6 and 7 from Vancouver in 2011 when it won the Stanley Cup.

"It's do or die, but we've been there before," Julien said. "Our goal now is to force a Game 7, but to do that you've got to win Game 6."

The Hawks held the Bruins to 5 shots in goal in the second period.

"It's been a war. It's been a battle," Quenneville said. "It's every game, every shift you're fighting for every kind of shift around the ice. You look at every minute from Game 1 to where we're at today, it's been an amazing series, and relentless hockey. I commend the guys on both teams for leaving it out on the ice." ■

Boston goaltender Tuukka Rask watches the puck fly past his right foot as Patrick Kane's second-period shot gave the Blackhawks a 2-0 lead in Game 5. (John Starks/Daily Herald)

40
VAUGHN

STANLEY CUP FINAL, GAME 6

JUNE 24, 2013 • BLACKHAWKS 3, BRUINS 2

A THRILLING, FITTING ENDING

Hawks Grab Cup in Stunning Fashion

By Tim Sassone

When you start your season 21-0-3, this is the only way it can end, by winning the Stanley Cup.

The Blackhawks lived up to the lofty expectations their spectacular regular season placed on their shoulders Monday night by stunning the Boston Bruins 3-2 at TD Garden in Boston to capture their second Stanley Cup championship in four seasons.

Bryan Bickell and Dave Bolland scored 17 seconds apart in the final 1:16 of the third period in one of the most stunning endings in Stanley Cup history.

Bickell poked in a pass from Jonathan Toews at 18:44 and Bolland scored during a scramble at 19:01 and — poof — instead of getting ready for a Game 7 on Wednesday, the Hawks were hoisting the Cup.

Patrick Kane, whose 2 goals in Game 5 were a key to the Cup win, won the Conn Smythe Trophy as MVP of the playoffs.

"It's an unbelievable feeling," said Hawks goalie Corey Crawford. "I don't know how many times we played for the Stanley Cup in road hockey or whatever. Everyone battled together, every guy in that room was behind each other and never got down."

The Bruins weren't going to go down without a fight, and they didn't.

It was Boston getting a late goal from Milan Lucic that had the Bruins looking forward to a Game 7. Lucic was left untouched in front of the net with 7:49 to play to score what appeared was going to be the winning goal.

But then lightning struck in the form of 2 Hawk goals in 17 seconds.

"I don't think you can call that," Toews said. "We knew we needed just one bounce there. Obviously, that was a big goal by them there to go up 2-1. You never know what can happen. This is a nice finish not having to go back to Chicago."

Toews made the pass across to a wide-open Bickell for his ninth goal of the playoffs.

"Tazer just got it in front and I just buried it," Bickell said. "What a roller coaster that was to finish it off the way we did. With this group of guys, it was a great season and it couldn't have ended better.

"We threw everything at them. We were sitting on the bench saying we're going back home for Game 7, but we never gave up. We got guys in front and good things happened."

On Bolland's goal, Johnny Oduya got the puck to the net and Bolland finished the play sending the Garden into dead silence.

"It was a huge goal and I give it to the defense and the team," Bolland said. "It went back to (Oduya), he shot it and I put it in.

Dave Bolland celebrates after scoring the second of the Blackhawks' two goals late in the third period. Bolland's goal proved to be the game-winner. (AP Images)

36
Reebok
STANLEY CUP
FINAL
36

"It was the best (goal) I ever scored; it's better than sex almost. As a team we battled hard to the end. The second Stanley Cup is always big."

There were eight Hawks around in 2010 when they won the first Cup.

"It's two different feelings," Patrick Sharp said. "It feels just as good. I'm happy to be part of the second one, too."

Hawks owner Rocky Wirtz was giddy as he praised coach Joel Quenneville and general manager Stan Bowman for the jobs they did this season.

"We want to be positioned to win every year, and we're going to do that every year," Wirtz said. "We know we can't win it every year, but if we get in position, that's our job. We want to be very, very good every year."

Toews was handed the Cup by commissioner Gary Bettman and quickly gave it to Michal Handzus and then Jamal Mayers, both first-time winners.

"What a great gesture by Johnny Toews and the captains," Mayers said. "It was amazing, an amazing feeling. I couldn't believe it. It was like a roller coaster. I can't believe it actually happened."

In all, there are 18 Hawks who won the Cup for the first time.

"I'm trying to hold back (the tears), but it's tough," said Andrew Shaw, who had blood running down his face as he spoke to reporters. "This is an unbelievable feeling. I've never experienced anything like it my entire life. I can't feel anything right now."

The Hawks were lucky to get out of the first period behind only 1-0. They were outshot 12-6 and hammered by the Bruins physically, yet trailed by only a goal thanks to the work of Crawford.

Toews scored an enormous goal at 4:24 of the second period just as the Bruins' third power play was expiring.

Racing down the right side, Toews beat Tuukka Rask to the far side with a blistering wrist shot to make it 1-1.

The Bruins got their only goal from Chris Kelly at 7:19 during a battle of fourth lines.

Rask said on the Bickell goal he was concerned with Toews behind the net.

"I think it was Toews," Rask said. "He had the puck and I had to respect him. I thought there was another guy kind of in the middle. Zee (Chara) was there, but the guy shot against the grain five-hole.

"The last one was just a deflection, post, and I got my stick there but not strong enough." ■

Patrick Kane (left) moves in toward the net during the second period of Game 6. (AP Images)

UMASS LOWELL
2013 CHAMPIONS
BOSTON BRUINS
STANLEY CUP CHAMPIONS 2011
beeken BIOMEDICAL
VAUGHN
VAUGHN

KANE AWARDED CONN SMYTHE TROPHY

Hawks Star Fourth American to Earn Playoff MVP

By Tim Sassone

Now with two Stanley Cups, Patrick Kane and Jonathan Toews have to be considered among the greatest Blackhawks ever.

Kane joined Toews in another exclusive club on Monday when he was voted the Conn Smythe Trophy winner as playoff MVP after the Hawks beat Boston 3-2 to win their second championship in four years.

Toews was the Conn Smythe winner the first time the Hawks won the Cup in 2010.

"It doesn't mean too much right now," Kane said of winning the Conn Smythe. "It's something no one can take away from you and as someone said, it's the fourth American to win the award.

"I'm blessed. I played with great players all playoffs and I wouldn't have been capable of doing this without my teammates. There are other guys that could have won it, too. You look at (Corey) Crawford, he probably got snubbed a little bit; Bicks (Bryan Bickell) and Sharpie (Patrick Sharp)."

The Hawks won the game with high drama, getting goals from Bickell and Dave Bolland 17 seconds apart in the final 1:16 of the third period to rally from a 2-1 deficit.

"My head is spinning," Kane said. "I don't even know what's happened the past 20 minutes, to be honest with you. You think you're going back for Game 7 and you score 2 goals to win it in regulation. This team has had the resiliency all year.

"You can't write the script any better. Two times in four years, there's something about this core. We've got to stay together because I think we can do some special things in the future, too."

Kane was emotional as he spoke to reporters on the ice.

"It's unbelievable to be in this situation," he said. "There were role players on the 2010 team that meant a lot to us that couldn't stay for us for the next year. I think nine or 10 or 11 guys got moved, and the Blackhawks did a great job of drafting and filling in those holes.

"You look at guys they drafted: (Brandon) Saad, (Andrew) Shaw, a big trade for (Nick) Leddy, who's going to be a big player in the future. And then just little signings like (Michal) Rozsival, picking up (Viktor) Stalberg, who's got great speed. We can go up and down the line and name off guys and how they contributed to this team and this game."

Kane had praise for Toews as well.

"He's a great player," Kane said. "He's played big in a lot of big games. He won the Conn Smythe our last playoffs and was awesome in that Olympic gold medal game and made some big plays tonight; a big goal, a big pass to Bickell to tie it up. He's just a competitor.

"That's really all you can say about Jonathan Toews is he's a competitor. He leads the team in the right way, and we all follow."

As for Kane, Brent Seabrook summed him up.

"Kaner is a guy that needs to play with the puck," Seabrook said. "We have a good D-core so we can give him the puck. When he's playing with the puck, he's so dynamic and skilled and fun to watch. Sometimes we watch him a little bit too much, but he's a great player and once he started to get it into gear he was going to be lights out. He was lights out in this series." ■

Patrick Kane hoists the Conn Smythe Trophy, awarded to the playoff MVP, following the Blackhawks' victory in Game 6 of the Stanley Cup Final. Kane led Chicago with 19 postseason points (AP Images)

STANLEY CU
CHIPOTLE
Hallmark Healt

29

LEFT WING

BRYAN BICKELL

Bickell Looks Back On Big Hit, Big Goal, Big Start

By Mike Spellman

After giving each other some good-natured guff about scoring overtime goals in playoff games, Bryan Bickell finally had to admit that, yeah, Patrick Kane's OT goal a few years back in Philadelphia might have been just a titch bigger than Bick's game-winner in the Stanley Cup playoff opener against Minnesota.

But Bickell's goal was still huge.

"The first game is the biggest game of the series — keep the home-ice advantage and also keep the momentum going," Bickell said.

"It's big for me to get that goal and give the team a jump."

His coach agreed.

"Bick's big goal, those are the types of things that happen in the playoffs," Joel Quenneville said.

But the game-winner in OT wasn't the only big thing the left winger provided this season.

His 128 hits in the regular season were second on the team and tops among forwards.

"That's part of my game; when I play my best is when I'm hitting," he said. "It gets me more into the game. It's fun."

Bickell finished the regular season tied for sixth on the team in points with 23, including 9 goals.

When the postseason started, few would have imagined that one of the guys carrying the Blackhawks to the Stanley Cup Final would be Bickell.

"He's one of those guys that maybe flies under the radar," Quenneville said.

But that's not the case anymore for the big guy who keeps adding to his legend. No longer is his locker visited only on occasion by the media; now he's surrounded by reporters after every game and practice.

Kind of wild, huh?

"I'm just having fun with it," Bickell said. "It's been a great playoffs for myself and I feel grateful to the team and, most importantly, just happy that the team is winning."

Bickell entered Game 5 against the L.A. Kings tied with Patrick Sharp for second in the league with 8 playoff goals. And there he was in Game 5 adding to his point total

Bryan Bickell, in a play typical of his style, checks Anaheim Ducks' Francois Beauchemin hard into the boards in the third period of the March 29 matchup between the two teams. (AP Images)

Reebok
29
BICKELL
29
Reebok
FROLIK
67
9

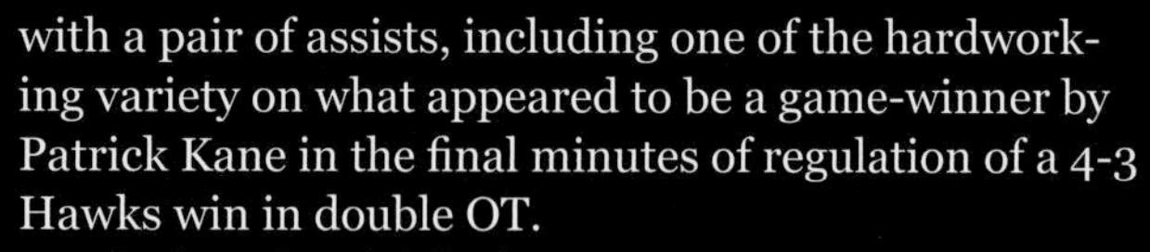

with a pair of assists, including one of the hardworking variety on what appeared to be a game-winner by Patrick Kane in the final minutes of regulation of a 4-3 Hawks win in double OT.

"I thought Bick had an amazing series," Quenneville said of the Western Conference finals. "We want him to keep playing like that. Sometimes you get called on it, but we don't want him to change much."

That should work for Bickell, who said the key to the season has been keeping in a routine and continuing the hard work.

"Just repeating in my head what works," he said. "If it's with Tazer and Hoss or Tazer and Kane, I have to go in front of the net. The puck's going to get there eventually either to give them a better opportunity to score or to give me an opportunity to score.

"I know I should've had a couple of more, but I'm happy for what's happened so far and I'm just trying to keep it up." ■

Above: Bryan Bickell celebrates with teammates after scoring a goal. (AP Images) Opposite: Though known for his bruising play, Bickell has soft, quick hands around the net as he shows against Edmonton Oilers goalie Devan Dubnyk. (Steve Lundy/Daily Herald)

OILERS
40
BAUER
CCM
BAUER
BAUER
SUPREME

50

GOALTENDER

COREY CRAWFORD

Grown-Up Crawford Leads Hawks to Final

By Barry Rozner

There is a fine line between arrogance and confidence in the NHL. And it's the finish line that often differentiates perception from reality.

Corey Crawford has carried the Blackhawks to the Stanley Cup Final.

"I think Corey is the guy for us," Viktor Stalberg said. "For some reason, he doesn't seem to get the recognition."

Crawford doesn't care, either, because he is a confident goaltender these days, prone even to saying that he expects to outplay the opposing goaltender.

He raised eyebrows when he offered before the Los Angeles series that, "I'm really looking forward to going up against (Jonathan Quick). We'll see who comes out of the next one looking this good."

It's arrogance if you don't perform. It's simple confidence when you do, and Crawford merely outplayed Quick — generally considered the best goaltender in the world.

"You've got to commend him on how he's played all year long," Hawks coach Joel Quenneville said. "I think the consistency, his approach where he just moves forward to see the next situation, the next shot. Unflappable in that area. Corey has been rock solid."

Crawford has hardly been flawless, but when he has made a mistake, he has bounced back immediately, a sign of immense growth in a goaltender who is not young in age (28), but who in regular-season games has played the equivalent of two NHL seasons.

You listen to him talk now and he doesn't resemble the guy who took the job away from Marty Turco two years ago.

You watch him walk now and he doesn't remind you of the guy who had to explain two huge postseason mistakes a year ago.

You look into his eyes now and he doesn't look anything like the guy who some thought was 1 bad goal away from losing his net in the postseason.

Quenneville used Ray Emery just enough to keep Crawford fresh and prod the No. 1 goalie just a tad, but Crawford is long past dwelling on the mistakes an inexperienced goalie makes, and he has total belief in himself and the total confidence of his teammates.

Corey Crawford outplayed more well-known netminding counterparts throughout the season and postseason. Here he makes a save against the Los Angeles Kings in Game 2 of the Western Conference Finals. (Steve Lundy/Daily Herald)

50
Reebok
Reebok
Reebok
Reebok

"It's never easy to get past those kinds of things," Crawford said of the overtime goals he allowed against Phoenix in April 2012. "But this is a different year, I'm a different guy and this is a different team."

After a bad goal in a crucial moment against Detroit, Crawford shook it off and stood strong.

"That's something I've learned to do better," Crawford said.

"You have to be able to move on quickly in this game and being able to do that sure has saved me a few times."

Crawford has never lacked for buoyancy, but poise is often a direct result of success — something Crawford knew he had to experience.

"I know that I can play great hockey. I'm sure of that," Crawford said following Game 6 against Phoenix in 2012. "There were a lot of ups and downs this year and I think you learn a lot from that. There's a lot to be gained from that process.

"I know I played better than last year at times, and I know I've got some things to work on, some issues to take care of. There's some things I have to do better and I'm disappointed in that. I could have been better in this series.

"But I know what I've got in me and I'll be working hard this summer to get better all the way around. I believe in myself and what I can do at this level."

So Crawford worked hard on remaining focused for 60 minutes — and sometimes more.

"I feel very confident," Crawford says now. "The thing is, I felt really confident last year. A couple times during games, I just got a little sleepy, but I learned from that and I made sure I was strong coming into this season."

Crawford may be the same goaltender, but he is unquestionably a different man, no longer questioning his place in the game or his spot on the Hawks.

He is a No. 1 goalie on the best team in hockey with a Stanley Cup.

What a difference a year makes. ■

Corey Crawford and Jonathan Toews keep a close eye on the puck as it trickles away from Los Angeles Kings left wing Dustin Penner during Game 2 of the Western Conference Finals. (Steve Lundy/Daily Herald)

50
Reebok

19

CENTER

JONATHAN TOEWS

Blackhawks MVP? It's Got to Be Toews

By Tim Sassone

Los Angeles Kings coach Darryl Sutter scrunched his face as only he can and pondered the question: Who was the Blackhawks' most valuable player, Jonathan Toews or Patrick Kane?

It was an important question considering the Hawks had the best record in the NHL at the time and would finish up with a Presidents' Trophy-worthy 36-7-5 mark. At the time, the race for the Hart Trophy for league MVP was all the talk.

Going by the pure definition of the award, most valuable to his team, it would have to be Toews, who finished with 48 points in 47 regular season games — just 7 points behind Kane — and finished up with a handful of game-winning goals, killed penalties on one of the league's top penalty-killing units and basically never took a night off.

"Jonathan impacts their locker room, maybe more so than his on-ice performance," Sutter said at the time. "Just what he brings them."

While Kane helped carry the Hawks early during their record 21-0-3 start and was dominating in some games, Toews made the team go with his tireless play.

"Other than what I think of our guy (Dustin Brown), he's the best captain in hockey," Sutter said flat out. "Think about it, he's already raised the Stanley Cup, so he's got it. Everything he does presents himself as the ultimate player. He is the consummate player."

Hawks coach Joel Quenneville concurred, just happy to have the two young stars on his side.

"I think Toews and Kaner have had years that deserve that kind of recognition and honor," Quenneville said. "Their consistency and contributions offensively, defensively and team-wise have been fun to watch. That's helped us have a lot of fun this year and a lot of success as well."

In the playoffs, though, Toews struggled out of the gate offensively, so much so that through his first nine playoff games he had gone without a goal and was reminded about it almost every day.

As the games continued, the goals never came and the losses to Detroit began to mount. Finally, in the second period of Game 4, Toews reached his boiling point after being sent to the penalty box for the third time in less than six minutes.

Just minutes before, the Red Wings had scored the eventual game-winner while Toews was in the box, and there he was again, and as frustrated as some have ever seen him, including Hawks defenseman Brent Seabrook, who skated over to have a word with the captain.

"I just tried to calm him down," Seabrook said. "We

A constant presence around an opponent's net, Jonathan Toews battles for a loose puck against Boston Bruins goalie Tuuka Rask in Game 2 of the Stanley Cup Final. (Steve Lundy/Daily Herald)

19
BAUER
BOSTON
C
19
WARRIOR
AUGHN

need him. He's the best player on the team and our leader. If the rest of the group sees him like that it's going to trickle down so we need him to be focused and be ready."

But in Game 5 against the Wings, the Hawks captain finally got off the schneid, beating Jimmy Howard for an important insurance goal in a 4-1 victory that kept the Hawks' postseason hopes alive.

"It's nice to see one go in," Toews told reporters. "You work so hard for so many games. Not only yourself, but your linemates, the guys that are out there with you. It builds your confidence. I don't care who you are. When you see one go in, you feel like you can do it again. That's the feeling not only with myself, but with our team right now." ■

Above: Jonathan Toews camps out in front of the Boston net during Game 2 of the Stanley Cup Finals. Opposite: Toews swoops into the Boston zone during Game 2. (Photos by Steve Lundy/Daily Herald)

FINAL
BAUER
BAUER
BAUER
TOTALONE NXG

81

RIGHT WING

MARIAN HOSSA

Hossa Thankful He's 'Back to Normal'

By Joe Aguilar

More than an NHL season was in jeopardy. So too might have been the career of a likely Hall-of-Fame player. Concussions severe enough to warrant exiting the ice on a stretcher provide that kind of threat.

Just ask Blackhawks all-everything forward Marian Hossa.

"You think about those things," Hossa said on the eve of the Stanley Cup Final. "You've got so much time on your hands that you start thinking about different things. It crossed my mind.

"But I knew when I was getting better; that was a good sign. I took my time, and I got back to normal."

Normal for Hossa?

Playing hockey at an elite level and, for the fourth time in six years for the 34-year-old Blackhawks winger, skating in the Stanley Cup Final.

Normal?

It took several months for Hossa to recover from the illegal hit to the head delivered by Raffi Torres in Game 3 of the Blackhawks' opening-round playoff series with Phoenix in the spring of 2012. Hossa's season was over — and three games later, so was the Blackhawks' run.

"I thought I was 'right' after the (Blackhawks) convention when I came here to work out," Hossa said. "But as soon as I was skating and started doing more exercises on the ice, I realized I was not myself yet.

"For me, it worked out that there was the lockout so I could take a couple of extra months to skate on my own and get in shape. I was doing the (stationary) bicycle and just sitting there, just pedaling."

When the lockout ended and the season started in January, Hossa was ready to resume his old form. His hot start coincided with his team's. He finished with Hossa-like numbers: 31 points (17 goals) in 40 games.

"He can make plays with the puck, he can score, he's got a great shot and he takes care of a lot of things defensively," said Patrick Sharp. "You've got the big Hoss man backchecking, stealing pucks and keeping plays alive. He's one of those special players that we're happy to have on our team."

One of the Blackhawks' elder skatesmen, Marian Hossa does it all for the Hawks on offense and defense. Here he crashes into Edmonton Oilers goalie Yann Danis. (Steve Lundy/Daily Herald)

HOSSA
81
81
Reebok
TOTAL ONE
CCM
CCM
Reebok
CCM
OILERS
EBERLE
14
14
14

If the Blackhawks win the Cup, Hossa could merit consideration for the Conn Smythe Trophy. Heading into the Cup Final, his 14 points (7 goals) in 17 games tied for the team lead with Sharp and Patrick Kane.

Big No. 81 has been a role model for his teammates, including 20-year-old Brandon Saad, who was 6 when Hossa made his NHL debut with Ottawa in the 1997-98 season. Hossa played for Pittsburgh and Detroit in the 2008 and 2009 Finals, respectively, before hoisting the Cup as a Blackhawk in 2010.

"It's been incredible," said Saad, who often skated on a line with Hossa during the regular season. "Watching him growing up, being from Pittsburgh and seeing him play in Pittsburgh, he's a phenomenal player. But you never (appreciate it) until you're around him every day."

"It's no fluke that he's been such a successful player in this league and has been playing for great teams," center Marcus Kruger said. "He's a guy that always works hard. He never takes a day off, basically. I think that's something everyone on our team can learn from."

A matchup with Boston meant Hossa got to go head to head against his neighbor, former Norris Trophy winner and fellow Slovak Zdeno Chara, he of the 6-foot-9, 255-pound frame. An injury sidelined Hossa for Game 3 against Boston, but he returned to help the Hawks win Game 4 on the road.

"I try to joke with him because he likes to be serious all the time on the ice," Hossa said prior to the start of the season. "I know he doesn't like to talk on the ice. I just try to tell some funny stories on the faceoff and hopefully make him laugh a little bit."

Hossa was just glad to be playing hockey again, and laughing. ■

Marian Hossa drives past Boston Bruins center David Krejci during Game 2 of the Stanley Cup Final. (Steve Lundy/Daily Herald)

81
CCM
Hossa
CCM

88

RIGHT WING

PATRICK KANE

Win or Lose, Hawks Love What Kane Brings

By Tim Sassone

Even when the Blackhawks suffered a rare loss during the regular season, there was a good chance Patrick Kane would be the best player on the ice. That was the case midway through the season when Kane scored twice and had an assist in the Hawks' 6-5 loss to the Edmonton Oilers at the United Center.

Kane led the Hawks with 55 points, scoring 23 goals with 32 assists in 47 games. Kane was plus-11 on the season

Kane seemingly had the puck all season, backing up his wishes to take his game to the next level with his play. He is more focused than he has ever been, more mature, and is having more fun playing the game he loves.

"I think I play better when I play creative, have the puck on my stick and am trying things," Kane said. "For me, I've got to be creative to play to my strengths, which are kind of skill and playing with speed and trying some things.

"For me, I have to play that way and have fun. I seem to play better when I have a smile on my face."

This season Hawks coach Joel Quenneville has seen a different Kane, now in his sixth season in the league.

"He loves the puck, and this year he seems to have it a lot," Quenneville said. "He's special. We don't want to take away his creativity.

"He's still willing to chip a few pucks in and unload it and make direct plays if he has to, but I think he's respectful of the score and time on the clock as well," Quenneville added. "I like that fact he wants the puck because when he gets it, it usually turns into good things.

"He's had the puck a lot more this year than he ever has, and he's quicker. He's shooting the puck well, and when he's on the ice he's a threat.

"I think he has improved defensively as well. His overall game, he's taken it to a different level."

After struggling in the first two rounds of the playoffs, Kane took it to a different level against the Los Angeles Kings in Game 5.

Patrick Kane led the Blackhawks in scoring in the strike-shortened 2013 season with 23 goals, 32 assists and 55 points. (AP Images)

88
BAUER
BAUER
88
BAUER
VAPOR

Kaner notched a hat-trick in the series-clinching win, scoring the game-winning goal in double overtime.

"I expected more from myself and my teammates probably did too," Kane said. "I just tried to get back to the basics — want the puck, go get the puck and try to make plays. That's kind of my attitude right now."

The Buffalo native is a big part of the Hawks' core that recaptured the feeling from 2010 when they won the Stanley Cup.

"The core players have gotten better, but if you look back to the year we won the Cup we had a lot of youth on our team and that made it more fun around the dressing room," Kane said. ■

Patrick Kane knocks Boston Bruins center Patrice Bergeron to the ice in the first period during Game 1 of the Stanley Cup Final. (John Starks/Daily Herald) Opposite: Kane tries to maneuver between three Red Wings during Game 6 of the Western Conference Semifinals. (AP Images)

88
BAUER
CCM
28
4
WARRIOR

HEAD COACH

JOEL QUENNEVILLE

Intimidating Coach Really Just a 'Big Teddy Bear'

By Tim Sassone

The scowl, the mustache, the steely eyes behind the bench — it's all part of what makes Blackhawks coach Joel Quenneville so intimidating. Or is he?

"He's a big teddy bear," said Hawks center Dave Bolland.

"Bolly? Really? Teddy bear? I've never been called that one before," Quenneville said. "That's surprising. Tough to comment on that one."

Quenneville was named one of the three finalists for the Jack Adams Trophy, which goes to the coach of the year.

Voted on by broadcasters, Ottawa's Paul MacLean and Anaheim's Bruce Boudreau were also named finalists.

"We're pretty happy with where we're at as a coaching staff," Quenneville said. "All the credit is reserved for the players and what they accomplished this year. You've got to commend them for the way they prepared themselves. It was fun being a part of it. You look back on certain seasons and the fun factor this year working with this group was over the top. It was a special regular season."

The Hawks finished with an NHL-best 36-7-5 record and 77 points and captured the second Presidents' Trophy in franchise history.

With Quenneville at the helm, the Hawks began the season with points in an NHL-record 24 consecutive games (21-0-3) and finished the year with a .802 points percentage, which was good for fifth best in NHL history.

The team's 77 points set a league record for the most points in a 48-game season, topping the 1938-39 Boston Bruins (74 points).

Quenneville is a player's coach who understands the needs of his players, from the many days off the Hawks get to short practices.

"It just shows his experience," captain Jonathan Toews said. "The reason why he has so many wins and has had so much success is he knows how to get the best out of his players. Whether it's the days off or whatever, he really gives us the opportunity to be ready for those games.

"Sometimes if we have an off night or we're flat and don't have that energy, he understands we don't need to go on the ice for an hour and a half the next day and figure out what the problem was. We just need to relax and go out and play better in the next one. A lot of our success comes from our coaching staff pushing the right buttons."

Quenneville won the Adams Trophy once before in 2000 with St. Louis.

The normally stone-faced Joel Quenneville lights up as he fields a question during a Stanley Cup Final news conference in June, 2013. (AP Images)

FINAL
NHL

"Definitely, I'm a lot more mellow than I was then," Quenneville said. "You've got to be ready to change and evolve a little bit, but at the end of the day you still have to trust your gut and feel for the game, trust your (assistants) and be adaptable."

Quenneville is 222-106-44 since coming to the Hawks early in the 2008-09 season. His .656 winning percentage is best in franchise history.

He also led the Hawks to the 2010 Stanley Cup, the organization's first in 49 years.

"For the years I've been here and the ups and downs I've had, he's helped me with my consistency level," said left wing Bryan Bickell, who also disputed Quenneville's tough guy image.

"You see him on the bench and he gets fired up after calls or with things that happen on the ice, but off the ice and in practice and in the dressing room, he's normal," Bickell said. "From what you guys see and from what we see, there are two different sides. He brings his game face, but that's just part of his game to get us fired up and such."

Bolland credits Quenneville with making him one of the top two-way forwards in the game.

"Since I've been here Q has been a great mentor to all of us," Bolland said. "I think he's helped my game and changed my game and kind of made me who I am.

"I think you guys see how he is on the bench and how funny it is when he gets mad, but it's all in good humor. He's just been great with us. He's been great with me, a great coach who has shown me a lot of the ways to do whatever things I have to do on the ice. He's always taking the time to show you so you know what your mistakes are."

Quenneville has won 660 games in his coaching career with St. Louis, Colorado and the Hawks, but he's never had a regular season like this one.

"I've been fortunate to have been on some nice teams," Quenneville said. "The challenges going into this season was we wanted to make sure our goals-against was a regular or normal number since last year it was abnormal. Making sure our special teams improved and getting off to good start was a point of emphasis.

"It was one of those years where it was almost on automatic pilot. You don't want to think it's that easy, but certainly things fell into place in a lot of good ways." ■

Joel Quenneville goes over strategy with assistant coach Jamie Kompon during Game 1 of the Stanley Cup Final. (John Starks/Daily Herald)

Reebok
29
CCM
FINAL
36

HAWKS OPTIMISTIC HEADING INTO OPENER

With Few Changes to Roster, Quenneville Expects Strong Start

By Tim Sassone

It might be pie-in-the-sky thinking, but to a man, the Blackhawks believed they had the pieces necessary to win their second Stanley Cup in four years.

"I'm sure a lot of teams are thinking the same thing, but we have to have that belief in this locker room, and I think we do," captain Jonathan Toews said.

The Hawks opened their 2013 season in Los Angeles confident that goalie Corey Crawford would rebound from a disastrous playoff, that Dave Bolland would be the answer as second-line center, that Andrew Shaw could hold his own at center on the third line, that their special teams would be improved, and that the size and toughness issues they had on defense last season had been addressed.

"We can definitely learn a lot from the last two years, you know, exiting in the first round, maybe having the potential to go a lot further but not quite putting the pieces together the way you have to (do) to have success in the playoffs," Toews said.

"It's a daily thing from now until the playoffs to try and improve on our team game and come together as a team and make sure that you're not necessarily overachieving but you're basically achieving your full potential as a team. If we do that this year, we can make a heck of a run at it."

Hawks coach Joel Quenneville wanted to make the playoffs before discussing any Stanley Cup runs.

"We like our team," Quenneville said. "We want to make the playoffs first. Once we get there we will be very happy with our team. We think we've got all the right ingredients, and we like the enthusiasm we've seen."

Defensemen Sheldon Brookbank and Michal Rozsival were the only two players on the roster who weren't around for last season's first-round playoff loss to Phoenix. Rookie left wing Brandon Saad had also made the team.

In this wacky, shortened 48-game, 99-day season, the Hawks hoped the fact they made so few changes will be an advantage.

"You've seen the last couple years we've had so many new faces, and this year it's kind of nice to see so many of the same guys back," Patrick Sharp said. "You can kind of build off what we accomplished last year. I know that losing out early in the playoffs wasn't any kind of accomplishment, but we had some big points in the season last year.

"We've been through the battles with each other so you can kind of build off that. I think the additions that were made are going to pay off big. I've skated with Sheldon since the lockout started and he has really impressed me. He's got

Duncan Keith gets a hand from Marian Hossa (left) and Brent Seabrook after scoring a goal in the home opener against the St. Louis Blues at the United Center in Chicago on January 22, 2013. (George LeClaire/Daily Herald)

Reebok
CCM
BAUER
A
7
BAUER

a lot more skill than I thought he had. He skates well, he moves the puck good, and we all know about his toughness."

Sharp saw all he needed to see of Rozsival in the playoffs.

"I remember Jimmy Hayes hitting him to end the playoff series there, hit him from behind, and I didn't feel too bad because he was a tough guy to play against," Sharp said. "For six games he was all over me. He was all over a lot of guys and really made it difficult to play out there.

"Again, you look at what he can bring to the offensive side of the game. He's got a great shot from the back end, he moves the puck well and he's been around. I think he'll be a great addition."

The shortened season was the wild card in all this. A great start is imperative, and depth and goaltending would be keys.

"The unpredictability this year is going to be very high," Quenneville said. "Every team feels like they have a chance to make the playoffs. A great example is after forty-something games last year, Minnesota was first in our conference and didn't make it at the end of the year.

"Everybody feels things can happen and they can happen quickly and they can change quickly. You want to make sure the depth we have been mentioning organizationally will get us through some of those challenges. We'd like to play four lines as much as we can."

Quenneville was optimistic special teams will be better. The Hawks finished 26th on the power play last season and were 27th in penalty killing.

On the power play, Andrew Shaw and Viktor Stalberg would get the first crack at filling the void in front of the net that was such a big problem last season.

The 5-foot-10, 180-pound Shaw is not your classic net front guy, but he has the intangibles the Hawks like.

"Both guys are capable of being that disrupter or distractor in front of the net with a quick stick, not just to tip pucks but make it a challenge for the goalie to find it," Quenneville said. "Shaw is capable of being there and being that annoyance that we're looking for. Maybe not the big body, but he has a way to find the right spot." ■

Andrew Shaw tries to punch one through Blues goaltender Brian Elliott during the Blackhawks' 3-2 win over St. Louis in the January 22 home opener. (George LeClaire/Daily Herald)

Reebok
SOBOTKA
17
17
17
Reebok

UNDEFEATED STREAK SETS NHL RECORD

Scotty Bowman Knows Just How Good Blackhawks Can Be

By Scot Gregor

Do the Blackhawks rate as an all-time great? Everyone seemed to have a take and their streak-stopping loss to the Colorado Avalanche shouldn't have swayed any opinions.

Sure, there were plenty of times during the first 24 games of the abbreviated season where it looked like the Hawks were never going to falter. But even while they navigated the first two-dozen games without a defeat, setting an NHL record in the process, you knew it eventually had to end.

Looking at the bigger picture, let's get back to how good the 21-1-3 Blackhawks were?

One opinion carried much more weight than any other, and it belonged to Scotty Bowman, who spoke exclusively to the Daily Herald during the Hawks' record run.

Not only is he the greatest coach in NHL history — by far — Bowman won a staggering nine Stanley Cup championships when he was behind the bench with the Montreal Canadiens, Pittsburgh Penguins and Detroit Red Wings.

More than anyone else, Bowman knows a powerhouse team when he sees one, and his 1976-77 Canadiens are widely regarded as the best in NHL history.

Still working at 79 as the Hawks' senior adviser, Bowman remembers Guy Lafleur, Larry Robinson, Ken Dryden and the rest of that remarkable Montreal crew like it was yesterday.

"I guess there are ways to judge teams," Bowman said. "Naturally, the records are magnified. If you're talking about the great teams of all time, in any sport, you look right at the record.

"With that Montreal team, we only lost eight games out of 80, and there were 11 Hall of Fame players on that team when it was all said and done.

"The Hall of Fame in most sports, there are mistakes for sure, but it's a pretty good barometer on the strength of a team."

The Blackhawks have some big-time talent in Jonathan Toews, Marian Hossa, Patrick Kane, Duncan Keith and Brent Seabrook, but Bowman said depth was the main reason this team made such a strong a run at all-time greatness.

"So many players have stepped up," Bowman said at the time. "They have a core of players, a fairly young core that's been there the last three or four years.

"But the defensive corps ... it used to be Keith and Seabrook would have to log between 26 and 30 minutes a game and they'd always

One big reason why the Blackhawks started the season with a bang was the emergence of young stars like defenseman Nick Leddy, shown here battling Los Angeles Kings center Tyler Toffoli for the puck. (John Starks/Daily Herald)

73
CCM
73
BAUER
8
Reebok
BAUER

have to play against the other team's No. 1 line.

"But now, the way coach (Joel) Quenneville has got it set up, if you look at the ice time of Keith and Seabrook and you look at the ice time of (Johnny) Oduya and (Niklas) Hjalmarsson, they're playing the same. I would say even strength, those four are playing equal minutes.

"Then you have (Nick) Leddy and his partner, (Michal) Rozsival, or sometimes (Sheldon) Brookbank, eating up 16-17 minutes a game. That's kind of unusual, that three pairs of defensemen are playing real close minutes at a pretty high level like that."

Toews, Hossa and Kane carried much of the scoring load early on, as expected, but Bowman said the Hawks' depth up front also has helped spark the fast start.

"If you notice, every time they take a penalty, if they're fresh, out comes (Marcus) Kruger and (Michael) Frolik. So you're not having to use your stars to kill penalties all the time," he said.

"When your main guys, when all of the responsibility falls on their shoulders every night, it's quite a strain. This is really a team."

The Blackhawks' incredible depth stretched down to the third line, where Andrew Shaw, Bryan Bickell and Viktor Stalberg combined for 18 goals and 18 assists early on.

And don't forget about the big contributions made by players such as Patrick Sharp, Brandon Saad and Dave Bolland.

"There's been an emergence of players," Bowman said. "Some of them didn't even hardly play last year, like Frolik. This year he's playing. Kruger's getting more responsibility, so is Bolland.

"Even though a lot of the players haven't changed, there have been a lot of changes in the way they've been used.

"And don't forget both goalies."

Corey Crawford and Ray Emery were solid in the net all season, combing to win the Jennings Trophy. They yielded just 52 goals in the first 25 games of the season.

When talk came to how the Hawks would respond to their first regulation loss of the season, Bowman thought they'd find their winning ways again ... and quickly.

"It's all about getting points in the bank, and they've been doing that," he said at the time. "And when you start a season like this, think about it, 10 of the first 12 on the road, a lot of things looked pretty tough.

"But when you get on a roll like that, you're not trembling and worrying about things like, 'How are we going to hold this lead?'

"The good news is when you have the points in the bank, things will even out a little bit. But at the same time, this team played 24 games in 47 nights and didn't lose a game in regulation. That's a heck of an achievement, especially in a league that's very parity oriented, you know?"

Scotty Bowman knew, and that should be good enough for any hockey fan. ■

In his second season with the team, veteran Johnny Oduya helped solidify a defensive corps that provided an optimal mix of speed and grittiness. (John Starks/Daily Herald)

20
CCM
BAUER
27
WARRIOR
FINAL

SEASON IN REVIEW

DOMINANT CAMPAIGN IN SHORTENED SEASON SET STAGE FOR THRILLING CHAMPIONSHIP RUN

By Daily Herald Staff

The Blackhawks were coming off back-to-back first-round exits from the Stanley Cup playoffs. A 113-day lockout threatened to cancel the 2012-2013 season before it even started.

After a tentative deal was reached on Jan. 6, a 48-game schedule was set, meaning the road to the Cup would be more of a sprint than a marathon.

Once the Hawks took ice, though, they never looked back.

Injuries to stars Marian Hossa and Patrick Sharp failed to derail a season that started with a record point streak and ended with the Hawks winning the Presidents' Trophy for best regular season record, the Clarence Campbell Bowl as Western Conference champs and then hoisting the Stanley Cup for the second time in four seasons.

Let's take a look back at the road to the Cup:

JANUARY (6-0-1)

The Blackhawks watched the L.A. Kings receive their 2012 Stanley Cup rings in perhaps the longest pregame ceremony in history and then went out and stole the show, scoring 3 goals in the first period and never looking back en route to a 5-2 win to open the season on Jan. 19.

Marian Hossa scored 2 goals and added an assist in his first game back from a concussion he suffered courtesy of Raffi Torres in the 2012 playoffs.

"It's huge for him to start with 2 goals," said Hawks captain Jonathan Toews, who had a strong game himself with a goal and an assist despite playing with the flu.

The Hawks opened the home portion of their season against the defending division champion St. Louis Blues and, behind Corey Crawford's 32 saves, made a bold statement in their 3-2 victory.

"I like the focus of our team right off the bat, the contributions we're getting from a lot of guys," coach Joel Quenneville said. "It's a positive start. We're happy, but let's keep trying to get better."

No problem there.

The Hawks avenged their playoff loss to Phoenix Coyotes the next night, and reeled off four more wins before losing 3-2 in overtime to the Minnesota Wild.

Dave Bolland readies to take a faceoff against St. Louis Blues center David Backes during the first period of the Blackhawks' home opener on January 22, 2013. (George LeClaire/Daily Herald)

BOLLAND
36
42
42
42
BAUER
Bauer
BAUER

The six straight wins to start the season set a franchise record.

FEBRUARY (11-0-2)

After losing a second straight game in a shoot-out, this time to the hated Vancouver Canucks, the Hawks went streaking again, winning four straight games.

Jamal Mayers and the Hawks paid back the Coyotes' Torres for his vicious hit on Hossa during the 2012 playoffs.

Mayers and Torres dropped their gloves early in the first period, setting the tone in a 6-2 victory.

"If that doesn't get you pumped up, nothing will," Patrick Kane told Comcast SportsNet following the first period. "That really set the tone for us and pumped up everyone. It gave you chills on the bench watching that."

The Blackhawks closed out a six-game road trip with a 3-0 win over Nashville, finishing the hardest part of their schedule 10-0-2.

"It was a great road trip from start to finish," Hawks coach Joel Quenneville told reporters.

Brandon Saad's third-period goal against San Jose made it 17 games without a regulation loss for the Hawks — setting the NHL record for the best start to a season.

The Hawks (14-0-3) broke a mark set by the 2006-07 Anaheim Ducks, who earned points in their first 16 games.

"It's nice to get another win and make history," Saad said. "Our group's had a great year so far, so we never expect anything less."

That was the fourth of seven straight home wins for the Hawks, whose point streak started to garner national attention.

"It's huge," Kane said. "For me personally, I'm a guy that has watched ESPN since I've been growing up and now you turn it on and it's one of the first stories, the Blackhawks and hockey, which you don't really see on that station.

"It's cool to see. Anything to get the game out there and see how we view it; we view it as the best game in the world, and hopefully other people will start seeing it that way too."

MARCH (9-5-0)

When the streak finally ended, it ended with a resounding thud.

Colorado manhandled the Blackhawks 6-2 in Denver, ending the Hawks' NHL record 24-game point streak to start the season and a franchise record 11-game winning streak.

"We should be very proud of what we accomplished," Quenneville said. "It was a great accomplishment from start to finish. We found some different ways to win night in and night out. Everybody contributed to something that hadn't been done.

"It's a great feather in our cap, but let's move forward here and try to get better as we go along. Certainly it was a lot of fun up until today and we should be proud."

The Hawks followed the loss in Colorado with a loss to Edmonton back at the United Center — one of only two times the Hawks lost consecutive games during the season.

The record point streak didn't put distance between the Hawks and Anaheim for first place in the Western Conference, though.

Anaheim closed to within 3 points of the Hawks after a 4-2 win on March 20.

Jonathan Toews tries to control a bouncing puck against the Edmonton Oilers in a midseason game. (Steve Lundy/Daily Herald)

BAUER
TOTALONE
TOTALONE NXG
CCM

With Marian Hossa and Patrick Sharp sidelined with injuries it looked like the race for the Presidents' Trophy would come down to the final days of the shortened season.

APRIL (10-2-2)

The only drama remaining in April was whether the Blackhawks would win the Presidents' Trophy.

The Blackhawks added Michal Handzus on April 1, Sharp and Hossa both returned from injuries and the Hawks went on another winning streak, taking control of the Western Conference race with 7 straight wins.

The Hawks clinched a playoff spot with a 5-3 win over Nashville on April 7 — becoming the first team to clinch a postseason berth.

"We obviously wanted to stay in the spot we're (at) in the standings," Toews said, "but first and foremost, our No. 1 goal coming in every season is we want to make the playoffs."

Mission accomplished.

The Blackhawks claimed the Presidents' Trophy for the first time since 1991 with a 4-1 win over the Oilers.

Toews and Kane finished the regular season tied for the team lead with 23 goals. Kane led the way with 55 points and Crawford and Ray Emery sparkled en route to capturing the Jennings Trophy, given to the goaltenders on the team with the fewest goals allowed during the regular season.

But the most important regular season number for the Blackhawks was their 36-7-5 record, good enough for home-ice advantage all the way through the postseason.

"The start of our year really put us in a great spot, but the consistency has been there, as well," Quenneville said. "I congratulate the guys. They deserve what they got." ■

Despite losing five games in March, Patrick Kane and his teammates carried on against the Western Conference to post the league's best record. (Steve Lundy/Daily Herald)

88
BAUER
88
8
BAUER

WESTERN CONFERENCE QUARTERFINALS, GAME 1

APRIL 30, 2013 · BLACKHAWKS 2, WILD 1 (OT)

HAWKS WORK OVERTIME IN PLAYOFF OPENER

Bank Shot and Backhand Win Game 1 for Hawks

By Tim Sassone

Maybe Blackhawks defenseman Johnny Oduya should try his hand at billiards when his hockey career is over.

It was Oduya's perfectly placed bank shot off the glass late in overtime that set up Bryan Bickell's winning goal in the Hawks' 2-1 victory over the Minnesota Wild on Tuesday night at the United Center in Game 1 of the Western Conference quarterfinals.

Viktor Stalberg chased down Oduya's pass that sailed over the head of a Minnesota defenseman as if planned that way and started a 2-on-1 with Bickell, who finished the play by tucking a backhander through goalie Josh Harding's five hole at 16:35.

"We talked about it a couple times that if we get time we can just take off," Stalberg said. "I saw them kind of seeing me take off and I didn't really see the puck.

"I was just skating, trying to find it somewhere and it kind of bounced down in front of me. I pulled up and found Bicks there. It was a great finish by him."

It also was a great finish by Corey Crawford, who rebounded from a tough early goal by Cal Clutterbuck to get the win.

Crawford was beaten cleanly to the short side by Clutterbuck's snapper from inside the left circle at 4:49 of the opening period on the first shot he faced.

"I lost it halfway and was never able to really see it come in," Crawford said. "It was tough to get over, but I was just trying to find a way to get myself back in the game. I was able to make a couple saves after that to really get into it and played solid after that."

Crawford made a point-blank stop on Zach Parise in overtime when it looked like the Wild might steal the first game.

"He was phenomenal," Stalberg said of Crawford. "I think we played good in front of him and kept their shooters to the outside, but there were a couple times when they got their Grade-A chances and he came up big.

"The biggest one was probably the one on Parise in overtime all alone in the slot. That's game change.

Patrick Kane goes down on one knee to field a difficult pass before releasing a shot on Wild goalie Josh Harding in Game 1. (John Starks/Daily Herald)

VAUGHN
VAUGHN
VAUGHN
WARRIOR
WARRIOR
KANE
88

"You've got to get a couple saves like that from your goaltender if you want to make it far in these playoffs. It was good to see Corey start this series on the right foot and hopefully he can keep gaining confidence."

Bickell was mobbed by his teammates after the winning goal.

"Stalberg has that speed and made it a 2-on-1," Bickell said. "The defense was late and Stalberg made a great play to get it to me."

Hawks coach Joel Quenneville praised all three players on the winning goal.

"That was a heck of a play," Quenneville said. "Johnny put it up there for a race, and Viktor used his great speed and saw the presence of Bick coming late with his speed. I think all three guys made really nice plays on it."

You would have thought the Hawks caught a break

Niklas Hjalmarsson (4) and Duncan Keith (2) defend against winger Jason Zucker as goalie Corey Crawford scrambles to his feet on the other side of the net in Game 1. (John Starks/Daily Herald)

before the game when Minnesota starting goalie Niklas Backstrom was hurt in the warmup and couldn't play.

That pushed backup Harding into a starting role, something he hadn't done since Jan. 30 against the Hawks when he failed to make it out of the first period after allowing 2 goals on 4 shots.

Harding was much better this time, stopping 27 of 28 shots by the Hawks through regulation and giving the Wild a chance to steal a victory. The Hawks had 6 shots in the first period but never seriously tested Harding.

The Hawks picked up their play in the second period and tied it on a power play at 2:06 on Marian Hossa's goal.

Patrick Kane set up Hossa's 37th career playoff goal by carrying the puck into the Minnesota zone and spotting his teammate flying down the left side. ■

WESTERN CONFERENCE QUARTERFINALS, GAME 2

MAY 3, 2013 • BLACKHAWKS 5, WILD 2

PICKING UP THE PACE

Hawks Have All the Answers in Win over Wild
By Tim Sassone

Blackhawks coach Joel Quenneville wanted his team to play at a higher pace Friday night in Game 2 against Minnesota at the United Center.

Consider Quenneville's message received loud and clear.

The Hawks had 48 shots on goal and stormed to a 5-2 win over the Wild to take a 2-0 lead in the best-of-seven first-round playoff series.

"There was clearly another level to their game tonight, and I'd say that there's at least another level to ours that was unfortunately in the wrong direction," Wild coach Mike Yeo said.

Michael Frolik and Patrick Sharp each scored 2 goals to back the strong goaltending of Corey Crawford.

"It's something we talked about," Quenneville said. "It was a very disappointing first period the other night. We were more on the receiving end and them scoring the first goal. We didn't dictate the way the game needed to be played as far as how fast we wanted to play. Tonight we were much more effective."

Frolik's first goal at 8:34 of the first period opened the scoring and was set up by Andrew Shaw.

It was the first goal of the playoffs for the hardworking Frolik, who made it 2-0 just 49 seconds into the second period when he scored short-handed from in front.

The goals came from another unlikely source, much like in Game 1 when Bryan Bickell's goal won it for the Hawks in overtime.

The Hawks' third and fourth lines were an important part of the team's success during the regular season and they're taking it into the playoffs.

"They've been huge all season and we know they're going to be even more important during the postseason," Jonathan Toews said. "They (the third line of Shaw, Bickell and Viktor Stalberg) did everything the other night. That's what we want all our lines to bring it like that."

Toews thinks the Hawks are tough to beat because they play any style and succeed.

"We like to think of ourselves as an offensive team that can create chances every which way," Toews said. "We can create chances off the rush and off shots from the point."

The Hawks dominated much of the first two periods and only some good saves by Minnesota

Patrick Sharp scored two goals in the Blackhawks' 5-2 Game 2 win. (Paul Michna/Daily Herald)

BRODIN
25
VAUGHN

goalie Josh Harding kept the score down.

Trailing 2-0, the Wild finally broke through against Crawford late in the second period as Devin Setoguchi took a pass from Mark Cullen and beat Crawford under the crossbar.

But Sharp responded with his first 2 goals of the series to make it 4-1.

"It's nice to score at home and it's nice to score in the playoffs," Sharp said. "Hopefully it's a start of many more."

It was another frustrating night for Minnesota's first line of Mikko Koivu, Zach Parise and Charlie Coyle, who have combined for 1 assist in the series.

Crawford stoned Parise five times on a power play midway through the second period with the Hawks holding a 2-0 lead.

"What a sequence there," Quenneville said. "Right there, all alone. That was a huge sequence there for him and for us and helped our penalty killers again."

Parise had 7 of Minnesota's 28 shots. Koivu took a pair of third period penalties in a miserable performance from the Wild captain. He was minus-3, as was Parise.

Again Quenneville won the matchup battle with defensemen Duncan Keith and Niklas Hjalmarsson out against the Wild's top line along with Toews, Marian Hossa and Brandon Saad.

Sharp broke through with a big insurance goal early in the third period when he beat Harding with a backhander in tight on an assist from Patrick Kane.

Kane made an even better pass to Sharp on his second goal that made it 4-1 — a no-looker from the slot to Sharp in the low left circle.

"I saw like three guys collapse on me so I just threw it to an area and was hoping he was there," Kane said. "He did a nice job of getting open." ■

Duncan Keith shadows Charlie Coyle while Corey Crawford makes a first period save in Game 2. (Paul Michna/Daily Herald)

Reebok
50
Reebok
Reebok
Reebok
Reebok
Reebok

WESTERN CONFERENCE QUARTERFINALS, GAME 3

MAY 5, 2013 · WILD 3, BLACKHAWKS 2 (OT)

WILD FINISH IN TWIN CITIES

Minnesota's Overtime Win Closes Chicago's Series Lead to 2-1

By Tim Sassone

From an optimist's point of view, the Blackhawks have to feel as if they took the Minnesota Wild's best punch and still got the game to overtime.

But it was the Wild pulling out a 3-2 win Sunday afternoon at Xcel Energy Center on Jason Zucker's goal at 2:15 of the extra period to make it a 2-1 series.

Knowing it had to be more physical if there was going to be any chance of winning the series, the Wild delivered in Game 3, outhitting the Hawks 34-13.

"It's part of the game and something we can do, too," Hawks captain Jonathan Toews said. "It's not the only part of the game that we didn't take control of tonight.

"Maybe they outhit us on paper, but there are a lot of other things we didn't do right that we have to get going if we want to win a game like this."

The Wild had a rabid crowd of 19,238 behind them — and they took advantage of it.

"It was obviously a difference for this team in their own building," Toews said. "They fed off the energy from their crowd and we didn't really respond. We let them do their thing through the second period and midway through the third, too.

"It wasn't until late in the game that we started really playing well and getting back to pursuing pucks and playing offense. The intensity really wasn't there."

Duncan Keith's goal with 2:46 to play forced the second overtime of the series. Keith blistered a shot past goalie Josh Harding from inside the left circle off a feed from Patrick Kane.

But the overtime didn't even last three minutes as Zucker beat Corey Crawford to the short side from the left.

"The guy got a quick shot off and I didn't pick it up right away," Crawford said. "It was just one of those ones that you think you have everything covered. It just got by me."

The Wild had taken a 2-1 lead on a goal by Zach Parise from Charlie Coyle at 3:09 of the third period. Coyle beat Michal Rozsival behind the net for the puck, which he fed to Parise in front for the backhander over Crawford's glove.

It was 1-1 heading to the third period thanks to Crawford and the Hawks' penalty killers, who were 3-for-3 in kills.

The Hawks opened the scoring at 13:26 of the first period when Johnny Oduya took a cross-ice pass from Kane and rifled a shot past Harding from inside the left circle.

The lead lasted until 1:30 remained in the first period when Pierre-Marc Bouchard put a backhander up and over Crawford on a rebound. ■

Corey Crawford blocks a shot by Minnesota's Torrey Mitchell. (AP Images)

BAUER
19
17
Minnesota
50
TOTALONE
EASTON
Reebok

WESTERN CONFERENCE QUARTERFINALS, GAME 4

MAY 7, 2013 • BLACKHAWKS 3, WILD 0

TAMING THE WILD

Crawford, Sharp Lead Blackhawks in Physical Game 4 Win

By Tim Sassone

Blackhawks goalie Corey Crawford got a lot of help from his friends Tuesday night.

Crawford made 25 saves in the 3-0 shutout of the Minnesota Wild in Game 4 of this Western Conference quarterfinal series the Hawks now lead 3-1, but his teammates blocked 26 more shots.

Led by Crawford, the Hawks killed all six Minnesota power plays.

"Our PK definitely won us the game tonight," Crawford said. "We blocked a lot of shots and we cleared pucks when we needed to. It was definitely a big effort."

Patrick Sharp scored 2 goals and Bryan Bickell had the third as the Hawks rebounded from Sunday's overtime loss.

The Hawks came into the game more concerned about what they had to do than anything Minnesota might try.

It was as if the Hawks needed to remind themselves the playoffs had started.

"Just to bring that playoff-style hockey," Hawks captain Jonathan Toews said. "We seem to kind of cruise out of the regular season. We were playing solid hockey and weren't making a lot of mistakes, but we didn't have that elevated level that you need in the playoffs. We've kind of carried that into the first three games.

"You watch every other series and see how tough it is on every single play and every single shift, little puck battles everywhere. Nothing is taken for granted. We've got have that same work ethic and same hatred for that team that they had for us last game."

Sharp's first goal came at 8:48 of the first period on a deflection of a shot by Michal Handzus, quieting the big crowd at Xcel Energy Center.

Sharp tipped Handzus' shot past goalie Josh Harding after Marian Hossa made a nice play along the boards.

Harding later hurt his left leg stopping a Toews drive to the net late in the first period and couldn't come out to start the second.

Rookie Darcy Kuemper, the Wild's third goaltender, replaced Harding and made his playoff debut. The first shot he faced from Sharp beat him to the short side at 1:02.

"I probably would have shot it no matter who was in net," said Sharp, who has 4 goals for the series. "I had speed coming over the blue line, tried to use their defenseman as a screen and just ripped one.

"Those pucks seem to find a way in more often than not. The fact that was his first shot, I wasn't thinking like that."

Johnny Oduya's 5 blocked shots led the Hawks, while Michal Rozsival had 4.

"We did an outstanding job blocking shots, clears, dangerous plays, big saves — it all goes hand in hand," Hawks coach Joel Quenneville said. "Our whole team game from the defense out was good, and Crow started it in net. Our team game today had much more bite to it."

Sharp stepped it up big time after Toews challenged the Hawks' best players in the morning.

"Of course we have a lot of depth on this team, but your best players have to be your best players," Toews said. "We know this series is a long way from being over, so those guys have to go out there and be better.

"First and foremost, I include myself when I say that. Guys like myself have to step up and be better."

Viktor Stalberg said the Hawks still can't take the Wild for granted even though the series is one game from being over.

"That's a very capable team," Stalberg said. "They've got some good players and a solid goalie, but I don't think we've been on top of our game yet. That's both a good and bad sign. We should be at the top of our game right now."

The Hawks were outhit 20-10, which was an improvement from Game 3.

"We're not going to be a team that runs around and kills guys left and right," Stalberg said. "We're more puck possession, so we're not going to get as many hits as some other teams because we have the puck more.

"But at the end of the day we need to be more physical." ■

Jonathan Toews swoops in on Wild goaltender Josh Harding in Game 4. Harding was injured on the play and left the game after the first period. (AP Images)

WESTERN CONFERENCE QUARTERFINALS, GAME 5

MAY 9, 2013 • BLACKHAWKS 5, WILD 1

VINDICATION

Hawks Overcome First Round Jinx, Finish Off Wild

By Tim Sassone

Consider it sweet vindication for Corey Crawford.

Even though the Blackhawks still have a lot of work to do, Crawford finally won the first playoff series of his career Thursday night at the United Center.

With Crawford making 22 saves, the Hawks eliminated the Minnesota Wild with a 5-1 victory in Game 5 to take the best-of-seven first-round series 4 games to 1.

Not only was it Crawford's first series win, it was the Hawks' first as a team since they won the Stanley Cup in 2010. They had been eliminated in the first round two years in a row.

"I think the past two years we felt we could have gone further, so this is definitely is a good start for us," Crawford said. "We didn't want to go back to their rink so we left everything on the ice.

"It's a win and we're moving on. It feels real good right now, but we've still got a lot of work ahead of us. For now we're going to enjoy it and rest up."

Crawford set the tone early by robbing Mikko Koivu in tight. That save drew the first chants of "Corey-Corey" for the night. There were several more to come.

"I definitely heard it," Crawford said. "It's nice and a good feeling. They've been hard on me at times this year, obviously, but that's a part of it. They expect us to be at our best, so it's only fair."

Despite winning the series in five games, the Hawks still don't feel they have played their best hockey. They had better crank their game up a notch or two in the next round no matter whom they get in the next round.

"We worked hard all season to get to this point," Jonathan Toews said. "Nothing is for sure, whether you're the first seed or the eighth seed. We worked hard to get out of that first round, but we know we've got to keep getting better."

Toews gushed over Crawford's play.

"What can I say about Crow?" Toews asked. "He was unbelievable. He was our best penalty killer making big stop after big stop. It's great to see the crowd get behind him.

"He's giving energy to the rest of our team and giving energy to the crowd and that's what we need — a nice, positive chant for Corey Crawford."

It was 1-0 after the first period and 4-1 after the second on 2 goals by Marian Hossa and

Bryan Bickell faces off with Matt Cullen in the Blackhawks' 5–1 win in Game 5. (George LeClaire/Daily Herald)

MINNESOTA
WILD
7
EASTON

the first career playoff goals by Marcus Kruger and Andrew Shaw.

Patrick Sharp got his fifth goal of the series on a power play in the third period.

"It feels pretty good," Sharp said. "It's been awhile since we won a playoff series here. Again, not really the best start. Crow made a bunch of big saves to keep it 0-0 and once we scored that first goal things kind of turned for us."

Hossa, who had a 3-point night, got that first goal, his second goal of the series, at 15:39 of the first period to open the scoring.

He took a pass from Toews in the low left circle and ripped a shot that went in off goalie Josh Harding. It was Toews' first point in the series after being blanked the first four games.

Harding was back in the net for the Wild after injuring his left leg early in Game 4, but he was pulled after Hossa's second goal at 6:26 of the second period made it 3-0.

The Wild was 0-for-2 on the power play and finished the series 0-for-17.

The Hawks' penalty killers have made all the difference in the series, led by Crawford.

Kruger's goal came at 3:19 of the second period with Shaw scoring just 35 seconds after Torrey Mitchell put Minnesota on the board.

"It was unbelievable to do it in front of our fans," Shaw said. "They deserve it. They've waited a long time for this through the lockout and everything." ■

Corey Crawford eyes the puck as Patrick Kane carries it to safety in Game 5. (George LeClaire/Daily Herald)

88
Reebok

WESTERN CONFERENCE SEMIFINALS, GAME 1

MAY 15, 2013 • BLACKHAWKS 4, RED WINGS 1

SAVING HIS BEST FOR LAST

Patrick Sharp's Play Key as Hawks Take Opener

By Tim Sassone

Patrick Sharp is saving his best for last.

The Blackhawks' veteran winger was all over the ice with a pair of assists and an empty-net goal in a 4-1 win over Detroit in Game 1 of the Western Conference semifinals.

Sharp did all the dirty work on Johnny Oduya's goal at 8:02 of the third period that snapped a 1-1 tie.

"Before the puck even came to me (from a Patrick Kane cycle), I saw Johnny break through," Sharp said. "I don't know what happened to the coverage, but it was a great play by Johnny to get open, and I just wanted to get it to him in his area."

Sharp has 6 goals in the playoffs, or as many as he scored during an injury-filled regular season. He also has 3 assists and is plus-6 in six games.

"I mean, it's playoffs, and I wasn't happy with the way things ended last year in the playoffs," Sharp said. "It's something I carried with me all summer and lockout and was really looking forward to the postseason.

"I don't care who scores or who gets the assists. It's all the same. You guys were beating up on me at the start of the year when I wasn't scoring and I was getting assists, and now you're telling me I'm great because I'm scoring.

"It doesn't matter who scores, our team is going to produce goals and whoever is doing it doesn't matter to us."

The Hawks dominated the second and third periods, outshooting the Red Wings 17-5 in the second and outscoring them 3-0 in the third thanks to a forecheck Detroit has no answer for.

"I don't know if they had their legs in the first period," Red Wings coach Mike Babcock said. "The first period was pretty even, but I thought they skated way better than we did in the second and third.

"I was hoping to come in here and steal this first game. I'm not taking anything away from them; they were better than us."

Detroit goalie Jimmy Howard made 38 saves to keep his team in the game.

"He had to be (good). We weren't good enough in front of him," Babcock said. "We gave up too many opportunities and made some key mistakes down the stretch."

Hawks goalie Corey Crawford had to make only 20 saves to win his fifth game of the playoffs. Damian Brunner scored on his own rebound in the first period and nearly had another goal in the third period when he hit the crossbar when it was still 3-1.

Blackhawks sniper Patrick Sharp celebrates after assisting on Johnny Oduya's goal in the third period of Game 1. (Bob Chwedyk/Daily Herald)

BAUER

Hawks defenseman Brent Seabrook bailed out Crawford by arriving just in time to swat Brunner's rebound out of the air before it could hit the ice and possibly bounce into the net.

"Crow made the initial save and it kind of felt like it was going in slow motion," Seabrook said. "It was spinning and luckily it hit the crossbar. It kept spinning down low and I just tried to get my stick on it."

Oduya's goal was his second of the playoffs. He finished the night plus-3.

"As the game prolonged I think we took over and put more pressure on them," Oduya said. "At that point it could have been anybody (scoring). I thought we had a lot of chances."

Marcus Kruger scored three minutes later to make it 3-1, beating Howard on a backhander into the empty net. Daniel Carcillo saved a whistle by batting the puck off the back of the net while Howard tried to freeze it.

The Red Wings had only 12 shots through two periods yet were very much in the 1-1 game going to the third.

Marian Hossa's power-play goal at 9:03 of the first period opened the scoring. Sharp stole the puck from Kyle Quincey along the boards and got it to Jonathan Toews, who fed Hossa in the deep slot for a quick snapper past Howard.

The Hawks' penalty killers, a perfect 17-for-17 in the first round against Minnesota, picked up where they left off against the Wild by going 3-for-3 in Game 1.

Pavel Datsyuk didn't have a shot, while Henrik Zetterberg had just 4.

"If you don't really have your legs, then you can't really get your game going," Zetterberg said, alluding to the fact Detroit had to play a tough Game 7 against Anaheim on Sunday.

"It would've been nice if we'd gotten one in on the power play there. We had a few chances but couldn't really find a way to score a goal." ■

Marion Hossa celebrates his first-period goal with his teammates in Game 1. (Bob Chwedyk/Daily Herald)

81
Reebok
88
TOTALONE NXG

WESTERN CONFERENCE SEMIFINALS, GAME 2

MAY 18, 2013 • RED WINGS 4, BLACKHAWKS 1

TABLES TURNED ON HAWKS

With Dominant Effort, Wings Even Series at 1

By Tim Sassone

The Red Wings turned the tables on the Blackhawks on Saturday, right down to the final score.

In a complete role reversal from Game 1, it was the Red Wings who dominated the second and third periods and seemed to be everywhere in a 4-1 win over the Hawks in Game 2 at the United Center that evened the best-of-seven Western Conference semifinal series at 1-1.

The Red Wings scored 4 straight goals after the Hawks' Patrick Kane opened the scoring at 14:05 of the first period.

"They had the puck a lot and we didn't," Kane said. "They kind of used our own game against us, playing puck possession, keeping it in. It felt like we were chasing the puck all the time.

"It's a lot of different things. It could be getting the puck back, but also when we do have it don't throw it away. It seemed like we did that a lot tonight, just kind of gave it right back. They regrouped with speed and came right back at us."

The Hawks managed only 20 shots on goal, getting just 5 in the second period and 7 in the third. The power play was 0-for-2 and looked mostly miserable.

"We knew they were going to come back and play much better than they did in Game 1 and obviously we didn't quite match the effort," Jonathan Toews said. "I wouldn't say it's a wake-up call. I think we know exactly what we need to improve on and we need to do it right away. There's no time to waste in this series. We know going into their building it's going to be more difficult than it was today."

The Hawks turned the puck over on 3 of Detroit's 4 goals, leaving goalie Corey Crawford to defend odd-man rushes on his own.

Damien Brunner tipped in a shot by Jakub Kindl past Crawford at 2:40 of the second period to make it 1-1, but Brendan Smith's goal at 16:08 of the second that put Detroit ahead to stay was a killer.

Defenseman Niklas Hjalmarsson fell at the blue line, allowing Henrik Zetterberg a clear path to the net. Then the Hawks lost Smith pinching from the right point with Zetterberg spotting him from the left of the net for the quick shot past Crawford.

"We made a few mistakes on the rush giving up pucks in the wrong areas," Toews said. "The last game we played smarter defensively and that was by holding onto the puck and making plays in their zone and keeping it out of the dangerous areas. We didn't do that tonight."

Hawks coach Joel Quenneville thought his team

played a strong first 10 minutes but couldn't sustain it.

"We didn't do what we were hoping to do over the course of the last 50 minutes," Quenneville said. "We've got to be harder in the tougher areas, particularly at their net. We didn't really look to shoot it. We seemed to be on the outside.

"We lost the momentum that game more by what we didn't do more so on our attack and in the offensive zone. I thought our game was way off as far as the pace that was needed and we weren't smart in certain areas."

The Red Wings return home for Game 3 confident they have made a series of it.

"Obviously we were disappointed that we didn't play the way we were capable of in Game 1 and so we went through it, had a look at it and felt if we just do what we normally do we'll be right here in a tight series and have an opportunity," Red Wings coach Mike Babcock said. "Good for us. It's a best-of-five now."

Detroit added to its lead with third period goals from Johan Franzen and Valtteri Filppula.

"This series is a long ways from over, I think," said Detroit goalie Jimmy Howard, who probably hasn't had many easier playoff games. "It was a totally different game.

"They were a lot better than us then (in Game 1)," Zetterberg said. "They skated a lot more and I think we just want to prove to ourselves that we could play a better game and we did." ■

Corey Crawford couldn't cover the net in time as Brendan Smith scores in the second period of Game 2. (George LeClaire/Daily Herald)

WESTERN CONFERENCE SEMIFINALS, GAME 3

MAY 20, 2013 · RED WINGS 3, BLACKHAWKS 1

UNFAMILIAR TERRITORY

Officiating Questioned as Red Wings Take Game 3

By Tim Sassone

For the first time all season, the Blackhawks have come face to face with some real adversity.

By losing 3-1 to the Red Wings on Monday night in Game 3 at Joe Louis Arena, the Hawks find themselves behind 2-1 in the Western Conference semifinals.

In Game 4, the Hawks face about as close as it gets to a must-win situation.

"We just have to dig down deep," said Hawks defenseman Duncan Keith. "Just because we haven't faced a whole lot of adversity this year doesn't mean we've never faced it in our lives before.

"Let's face it: Winning in the playoffs isn't easy. It's not always going to go your way."

Sometimes the calls go against you, which is what happened at 5:43 of the third period, just more than a minute after Patrick Kane scored to cut Detroit's lead to 2-1.

It appeared that Viktor Stalberg had tied it with a goal through a screen, but the referees wiped it out, ruling that Andrew Shaw was in the crease and interfered with goalie Jimmy Howard.

Replays showed there was no contact.

"We did everything we could to get the momentum back, and we did, but then we kind if hit the wall there after they disallowed the goal," Hawks coach Joel Quenneville said.

"I disagreed with the call. He didn't touch the goalie. It certainly did (change the momentum of the game). We're 2-2 and we had the momentum. We had everything going with some hits and offensive zone time. Obviously coming back from 2-0 that quickly you're in a great spot."

Pavel Datsyuk scored a minute after that to make it a 2-goal lead again for the Red Wings.

"I wasn't down there, so I don't know exactly what happened, but from what I saw I find it hard to believe that our player restricted the goaltender from making the save," Hawks captain Jonathan Toews said.

"The puck came from the same side and he was against his post, so I don't understand that one.

"Whenever you get a goal called back it's a frustrating thing, but give us credit. We stuck with it and worked hard. We know there's going to be some adversity; we know there are going to be some tough moments in these playoffs, and we just have to rise to the occasion."

Detroit coach Mike Babcock thought Kane's goal at 4:35 shouldn't have counted because of a hit from behind into the boards that Niklas Hjalmarsson laid on Johan Franzen.

While Keith picked up the loose puck and fed

Kane for the breakaway, Franzen was on the ice at the other end.

"It should have been a two-minute penalty," Babcock said. "But this is the way I look at it. Those referees are trying to get to the Stanley Cup Finals like the rest of us, and it's fast.

"When I go in and watch the replay and see that that's a penalty, they don't get to watch the replay."

The Hawks haven't lost three games in a row all season.

"I feel we played some real good hockey for three periods and just didn't score enough goals to win," Toews said. "That call goes against us and they come back and score — we were fighting all game, trying to get control of the game and never did."

Goals by Gustav Nyquist and Drew Miller 31 seconds apart early in the second period busted open what had been a scoreless game.

Nyquist scored at 7:49 when Damien Brunner flipped the puck high over Nick Leddy at the left point. Nyquist chased the puck down then cut around Brent Seabrook to beat Corey Crawford from a tough angle to the left.

Miller made it 2-0 at 8:20 after a turnover by Michal Rozsival, who was then beat back by Patrick Eaves. Crawford stopped Eaves' shot, but a diving Miller poked in the rebound.

The Hawks were 0-for-4 on the power play and looked mostly lost.

"We're not frustrated at all," Keith said. "Obviously, we want to score goals, but they do a good job on the penalty kill. For sure we'd like to get a goal on the power play. We just have to keep with it."

The Hawks outshot the Red Wings 15-9 in a fast-paced but scoreless first period. It might have been the best period of the playoffs for the Hawks, who were engaged and feisty.

"I thought we had more play in their end; I thought we had more predictability in our game," Quenneville said. "We didn't get slowed down in certain areas, but we're going to have to be better than we were today. We were certainly a lot better today." ■

Gustav Nyquist tries to slow down Brandon Saad as Jakub Kindl (4) looks on during the first period of Game 2. (AP Images)

WESTERN CONFERENCE SEMIFINALS, GAME 4
MAY 23, 2013 • RED WINGS 2, BLACKHAWKS 0

FRUSTRATION BUILDS

Blackhawks in Deep Hole after Suffering First Three-Game Losing Streak

By Tim Sassone

The Red Wings have managed to frustrate Jonathan Toews and the Blackhawks like no other team has done all season.

Goalie Jimmy Howard and the Red Wings pushed the Hawks to the brink of elimination with a 2-0 win in Game 4 of the Western Conference semifinals at Joe Lewis Arena.

Howard made 28 saves while Corey Crawford made 26, failing to stop only Jakub Kindl's shot on a power play in the second period. Dan Cleary added an empty-net goal with Crawford pulled for a sixth attacker.

It was the first power-play goal allowed by the Hawks in the playoffs.

The goal came with Toews serving 1 of the 3 penalties he took in the second period alone. He disputed the high stick call against Justin Abdelkader that the Red Wings scored on.

Abdelkader did a great job of selling it to the officials.

"Obviously, I'm disappointed by a few of the calls, but it was in the heat of the moment," Toews said. "It doesn't help our team. I still think we played hard and found a way to stay in the game. We played our tails off and did a lot of good things. We just couldn't find the back of the net."

Someone asked Toews if he felt he became unglued.

"I wouldn't take it that far," Toews said. "Emotions run high in these games and my stick got a little loose there. I was playing hard and sometimes that happens.

"You can point the finger at whatever you want. We're getting shots; we're getting chances. We hit a bunch of posts again tonight. They're just not going in."

So are the Red Wings frustrating Toews, who has yet to score a goal in the playoffs?

"You'll have to ask Joel (Quenneville)," said Red Wings coach Mike Babcock. "We're too busy worrying about our own focus."

Quenneville wouldn't blame Toews for losing his cool.

"I thought Tazer, he worked," Quenneville said. "A couple penalties there, the first two, you could argue about. We couldn't get him to the

Red Wings goaltender Jimmy Howard stops a shot by Jonathan Toews in the second period. The Red Wings frustrated the Blackhawks throughout Game 4. (AP Images)

Reebok
TOEWS
19
VAUGHN

bench; he had six minutes in a row there.

"You lose a little momentum there, but he's a battler. Johnny had some chances, he had some looks."

The power play again was miserable, going 0-for-3.

"We can get better on it," Patrick Sharp said. "We need to get more pucks to the net, play with more intensity. We've got to find a way to come up with something, whether it's scoring chances or goals. We just have to be better."

The Red Wings made an adjustment on their power play, and it paid off in their first goal of the series.

"We adjusted our power play yesterday and got Mule (Johan Franzen) off the net and told him to shoot it," Babcock said.

Kindl scored on a long shot from the left side past Crawford through an Abdelkader screen. ■

Above: Michal Handzus squares off with Brendan Smith in the second period. Opposite: Jonathan Toews crashes into Red Wings goaltender Jimmy Howard as the Red Wings seemed to have the Blackhawks corralled in Game 4. (AP Images)

BAUER
BAUER
19
C
19

WESTERN CONFERENCE SEMIFINALS, GAME 5

MAY 25, 2013 • BLACKHAWKS 4, RED WINGS 1

HAWKS TURN ON THE POWER

Toews, Shaw Score with Man Advantage to Keep Hawks Alive

By Tim Sassone

All was well for the Blackhawks on Saturday night as they lived to play another day.

The power play finally contributed with 2 big goals, 1 of them by Jonathan Toews, his first of the playoffs, in a 4-1 win over Detroit that forced a Game 6 on Monday at Joe Louis Arena.

Andrew Shaw added 2 goals, including 1 on the power play, keeping the Hawks alive in the best-of-seven Western Conference semifinals.

"We had a great season and we didn't want to see it end like this," Shaw said. "We tried to pump each other up and we came out hard in the first period and created momentum through the game and just took off with it.

"We finally got the power play going and Johnny scored a goal. It was awesome. They've been all over him, but it just shows he's a great captain. He sticks with it and was rewarded tonight."

The power play came up big in short span in the second period, scoring twice to break open a 1-1 game at the United Center.

"They were better than us today," said Detroit captain Henrik Zetterberg. "That's a fact."

Shaw scored the go-ahead goal at 13:08 when he tipped in a Duncan Keith shot from near the blue line. The Hawks had control of the puck for more than a minute after Toews won a faceoff.

Toews scored himself on another power play at 15:47 after Justin Abdelkader cross-checked Patrick Kane.

Toews roofed a shot over Jimmy Howard from the short side for his first goal of the playoffs in his 10th game. Toews leapt into the arms of Marian Hossa after finally scoring.

"To see Jonathan get his first, it's nice to see that smile on his face instead of a frown," Bryan Bickell said. "It's good for him. He got that first one and there's many more to come."

Bickell not only opened the scoring at 14:08 of the first period with his fourth goal of the playoffs from in the slot, he set a physical tone before that with a huge hit on Joakim Andersson.

"I feel like that's part of my game," said Bickell, who laid out Niklas Kronwall in the third period with another thunderous hit. "Get the crowd into it, you know? Slow them down any way possible. That's what my game is all about."

Andrew Shaw and the rest of the Blackhawks elevated their play in Game 5. Shaw battles for position with Niklas Kronwall in the second period. (AP Images)

Reebok
CCM
65
55
35
VAUGHN

After Dan Cleary tied it at 9:37 of the second period on a rebound, the Hawks' power play went to work and decided the game on goals by Shaw and Toews.

"He (Shaw) made a nice tip there in front of the net," Keith said. "It's the screen that we need and the shot. It's not rocket science. It's moving the puck around and taking what they give you. We did that tonight."

The Red Wings still lead the series 3-2, but the Hawks think they might have wrestled back the momentum.

"We have to go back to Detroit and win a game," Hawks coach Joel Quenneville said. "I just thought today we got the momentum back on our side and let's go in there and keep it."

Said Keith: "We want to keep it going. We feel good right now, we feel like we played the way we know we can and skated the way we can. The power play gave us a boost though for sure."

Brent Seabrook and Keith were reunited on defense and the move by Quenneville paid off. Seabrook played his best game of the series with an assist, 7 shots and 2 hits in 23:20 of ice time.

That's more than double the ice time he received in Game 4.

"I was pretty nervous before the game started, to be honest," Seabrook said. "(Keith) calms me down out there. I think we get yelling at each other every once in a while and that sort of takes my focus off thinking too much — just get (ticked) off at him and I just play.

"I can't think too much. I feel I get myself in a rut so tonight I just went out there and played." ■

Bryan Bickell tracks down the Red Wings' Johan Franzen in the first period of Game 5 of the NHL Western Conference Semifinals. Bickell had a goal on three shots in the game. (AP Images)

Red Wings
BAUER
WARRIOR
EAGLE
WARRIOR
EASTON
Reebok

WESTERN CONFERENCE SEMIFINALS, GAME 6

MAY 27, 2013 • BLACKHAWKS 4, RED WINGS 3

NEVER SAY DIE

Blackhawks Rally in Third Period to Force Game 7

By Tim Sassone

It was going to be another long off-season for Corey Crawford.

As well as Crawford has played in these playoffs, he was going to be remembered for the one he didn't catch Monday night at Joe Louis Arena — Joakim Andersson's floater that sailed over Crawford's glove at 10:11 of the second period to snap a 1-1 tie.

But Crawford's teammates bailed him out with a stunning 3-goal, third-period rally for a 4-3 victory that forced a seventh and deciding game in the Western Conference semifinals.

Michal Handzus scored 51 seconds into the third period to tie it before Bryan Bickell scored the go-ahead goal at 5:48 on a pass from Jonathan Toews.

Michael Frolik scored on a penalty shot at 9:43 to make it 4-2. Frolik became the first player in NHL history to score 2 penalty shot goals in the playoffs.

"I lost it," Crawford said of Andersson's goal that Red Wings coach Mike Babcock called a gift. "It's a brutal one, obviously, but I was able to rebound after that. I just told myself it can't get worse than that and to come up with the next save."

Handzus was left all alone in front to beat goalie Jimmy Howard less than a minute into the third period. Niklas Hjalmarsson found him with a backhand pass from along the wall, and Handzus had plenty of time to pick his spot.

"We were down 1 goal and usually we try to pinch as defensemen and throw the puck at the net," Hjalmarsson said. "He did a good job getting in front of the net there and waited for the goalie to go down.

"It was a huge momentum goal because we kind of took over the game for a little bit. I don't think any player has been alone for that long throughout the whole series."

Bickell outworked Brendan Smith in front for his fifth goal of the playoffs, swatting home a feed from Toews.

Frolik scored on his penalty shot at 9:43 of the third on a move nobody had seen before. Frolik came in on Howard with speed and backhanded the puck high into the net.

"This year during the lockout I was successful in the Czech (League) doing it in the shootouts," Frolik said. "It was kind of my move, and I'm glad it worked out."

Frolik said he was a little surprised to get the penalty shot call after he was whacked on his hand on a breakaway.

"I tried to do my move and he hit me on the

Marian Hossa celebrates after scoring against his former team in the first period of Game 6. (AP Images)

Kroger
Reebok
CCM
NHL

hand and kind of lost it," Frolik said. "It wasn't a big hook or a big slash, but I felt his stick on my hand and the referee called it."

There were no rah-rah talks in the dressing room before the third period, just a feeling of being positive.

"It was just pure confidence and our heads were in the right spot," Toews said. "We knew what we had to do and we weren't panicking."

The quick goal by Handzus was exactly what was needed.

"There was no negative talk," Bickell said. "The talk was all positive. We felt if we stuck with our game we could do it. Coming on the ice we felt confident and took over.

"Getting that first goal by Zeus was huge. I felt when we got that goal it got us fired up to carry on."

The Hawks now have all the momentum in the series going home for their first Game 7 since losing to Vancouver in overtime in 2011.

"We feel all our hard work is paying off," Toews said. "We're finding ways and doing the right things to score goals and we're confident when we get those chances they're going to go in."

The Hawks actually opened the scoring on Marian Hossa's power-play goal at 3:53 of the first period. Hossa fought off a check to tap in a Toews rebound for the Hawks' third power-play goal in the last two games.

The net became dislodged while the puck was crossing the line, but a video review upheld the goal.

It stayed that way until nearly a minute remained in the period when Patrick Eaves scored on a rebound with 1:09 to play.

"We made some young mistakes in the third period and they ended up in our net," Babcock said. "I think tonight gave us a sense of confidence. It's not like they came in here and squashed us or anything. They got what we gave them tonight.

"I think if I would have told Detroit, Michigan, before this series that we were going to play Chicago in Game 7, I think everybody would have been pretty excited. I love Game 7s. We got a chance to push them out of the playoffs." ■

Carlo Colaiacovo (28) tries to clear the puck from Marcus Kruger (16) in the first period of Game 6. (AP Images)

16
EASTON
16
FOX
EASTON

WESTERN CONFERENCE SEMIFINALS, GAME 7

MAY 29, 2013 • BLACKHAWKS 2, RED WINGS 1 (OT)

HISTORIC CARDIAC COMEBACK

Seabrook's Overtime Goal Lifts Blackhawks in Game 7

By Tim Sassone

Brent Seabrook has scored bigger goals before this — all of them in his driveway as a kid growing up in British Columbia.

It was Seabrook's goal at 3:35 of overtime Wednesday that gave the Blackhawks a 2-1 win over the Red Wings in Game 7 of the Western Conference semifinals at the United Center.

Seabrook's shot deflected off defenseman Niklas Kronwall's skate and past goalie Jimmy Howard to send the Hawks into the West finals against Los Angeles.

"Shooting pucks around in the front yard, against the garage, breaking garage doors, it's always something you think about, scoring an overtime winner in Game 7," Seabrook said. "I love overtime. I think it's exciting and lots of fun. The stakes are really high."

Seriously, it was the biggest goal of Seabrook's career.

"I don't think I've scored a bigger goal than that," he said. "With the Game 7 mentality, in overtime, against Detroit, it was pretty special."

Dave Bolland started the play with a hard check on Gustav Nyquist along the boards, and the puck squirted free to Seabrook — who took a few strides inside the blue line and fired a wrist shot.

"I just tried to get it on net and get it past Kronwall," said Seabrook. "I didn't want to get it blocked.

"I don't even know if I saw it go in, to be honest. I just heard the horn going and the boys jumping out. It was a pretty exhausting game, but I think I was more tired during the celebration. You don't get to do that too many times, and it'll be something I'll remember for the rest of my life."

The shot made a deserving winner out of goalie Corey Crawford, who was sensational with 26 saves. Crawford was beaten only by Henrik Zetterberg on a shot he had no chance to stop 26 seconds into the third period that made it 1-1.

"After that goal (by Seabrook) it's a little of a relief, but it's more a reward from our hard work and from us being relentless," Crawford said. "It feels great. Obviously, it's another step for us to move on to our ultimate goal."

"The real dream is two more rounds from now," Seabrook said.

The game wasn't free of controversy.

It appeared that Niklas Hjalmarsson had scored with 1:47 left in regulation to snap the 1-1 tie, but referee Stephen Walkom waved if off because he had called a pair of penalties well behind the play.

Jonathan Toews battles Detroit's Niklas Kronwall for position in front of the net in Game 7. (Steve Lundy/Daily Herald)

VAUGHN
BAUER
19
VAUGHN
19
TOEWS 19
55
Red Wings

Walkom sent off both Kyle Quincey and Brandon Saad for roughing, even though it was Saad who got mugged in front of the Detroit bench.

"I didn't agree with it, but there's not much you can do," Saad said. "I was shocked when the linesman told me I was going to the box."

None of the Hawks agreed with the call to wipe out the goal.

"That was a tough call," Patrick Kane said. "It was a tough break for us, but we wanted to regroup and get back at it in overtime."

The win completed the comeback from 3-1 down in the series for the Hawks.

"I think we might have needed a little adversity to get us going here in the playoffs the last three games," Kane said. "It's a fun time to be a Blackhawk. The city's got to be buzzing right now. We have a great opportunity to do something special."

The Red Wings dominated the third period after getting the tying goal from Zetterberg.

"They came flying out of the gate in the third period and made a nice play to get their goal," Crawford said. "It was just a matter of cooling down, not losing our cool or lose our heads."

The Hawks took a 1-0 lead into the third period thanks to a Patrick Sharp goal and Crawford's amazing play.

It was scoreless until 1:08 of the second period when the Hawks caught the Red Wings in a bad line change and capitalized on a 3-on-1, with Sharp scoring his seventh goal of the playoffs on a nice passing play with Michal Handzus and Marian Hossa.

The Red Wings played most of the game without Valtteri Filppula, who hurt his ankle in a first-period collision with Andrew Shaw.

"Obviously, I was disappointed we lost Filppula early," Red Wings coach Mike Babcock said. "I thought we could've been a lot more dynamic if we'd had Fil.

"Obviously, they're a very talented group and I thought we pushed them real hard in the series and had a lot of fun doing it. Those dreams you have as a kid in Game 7, you always score. The other team doesn't score." ■

Corey Crawford smothers the puck during the epic Game 7 overtime thriller. Crawford totaled 26 saves on the night. (Steve Lundy/Daily Herald)

26
CCM
Reebok
Reebok
Reebok

WESTERN CONFERENCE FINALS, GAME 1

JUNE 1, 2013 • BLACKHAWKS 2, KINGS 1

FIRST THINGS FIRST

Sharp, Hossa and Hawks Take 1-0 Series Lead

By Tim Sassone

It was a crazy first period for the Blackhawks on Saturday.

The Hawks trailed the Los Angeles Kings 1-0 despite outshooting them 17-2.

And they were pleased.

"We liked the way we played," Hawks coach Joel Quenneville said. "It was kind of an injustice being down 1-0, but we exited the bench with a positive approach. We made them play in their zone.

"Trying to get their defense to turn and play in their end is something we want to establish. If you make them play in their end you can wear them down, you can get chances and get shots."

It paid off for the Hawks in the second period when they got goals less than four minutes apart from Patrick Sharp and Marian Hossa and held on to beat the Kings 2-1 at the United Center in Game 1 of the Western Conference finals.

Both goals were straight out of the textbook on how to beat Kings goalie Jonathan Quick as Sharp scored on a rebound and Hossa on a tip-in from in front.

"He's a good goalie. We all know that, and when he sees pucks he's going to stop them," Sharp said. "So anytime you can get those second and third chances, drive to the net and get to the inside, that's the idea."

The Hawks then turned it over to Corey Crawford, who made 20 straight saves after allowing a fluky goal to Justin Williams in the first period.

The Hawks played the last 1:41 of the game on the power play after Jeff Carter tripped Dave Bolland in retaliation for a questionable hit Bolland put on Mike Richards behind the Hawks' net moments earlier.

Bolland appeared to leave his skates to hit Richards on the chin with his shoulder, but referees Wes McCauley and Dan O'Halloran kept their whistles in their pockets.

Kings coach Darryl Sutter had no problem with the hit because he couldn't see what happened.

"Couldn't see anything," Sutter said. "He was behind the net and behind the goalie and with guys changing, I really couldn't see it."

The Hawks played keepaway on the power play and never let Quick get out of the net for a sixth attacker.

"We were up by 1 goal and just wanted to be smart with the puck," Hawks defenseman Duncan

Corey Crawford comes up with a big save in second-period action during Game 1. Crawford outplayed the Kings' more celebrated goalie, Jonathan Quick, in the series. (Bob Chwedyk/Daily Herald)

Reebok
Reebok
Reebok

Keith said. "I though we moved it around the way we wanted to there, just trying to be a little conservative and protect our lead."

It might have been the most important Hawks power play of the playoffs.

"It was exactly what we wanted to do," said Hawks winger Patrick Kane. "Move it around and keep it away from them. We've seen before where that can kind of haunt you where if you do something stupid and they intercept a pass, they can come down and score."

The Hawks never let the bigger and more physical Kings get their forecheck going, controlling the puck for much of the game.

"It's something we talk about, trying to have good breakouts and it helps when our forward come back and do a good job supporting us," Keith said. "L.A is a good forechecking team and they have a lot of guys who get in there hard, so it's not easy."

The Kings are now 1-6 on the road in the postseason after going 10-1 last season away from the Staples Center when they won the Stanley Cup.

While the Hawks got goals from Sharp and Hossa, and Jonathan Toews was noticeable in 17 strong minutes, the Kings got little from their top players.

Anze Kopitar had 1 shot in 19 minutes, and Dustin Brown had no shots. Carter was minus-1 with 1 shot, and Richards had just 1 shot. Defenseman Drew Doughty was minus-2.

"I think the two guys that scored for them are going to score goals," Sutter said. "We have guys that have to score goals, and that's how close it will be."

Sharp scored at 12:29 on a Johnny Oduya rebound for his eighth goal of the playoffs. Hossa made it 2-1 at 16:22 with his sixth goal, a tip-in of a Keith shot from the left point. ■

The Blackhawks gather around Corey Crawford after Chicago's Game 1 win. (Bob Chwedyk/Daily Herald)

SEABROOK
7
ODUYA
27
Reebok
WARRIOR

WESTERN CONFERENCE FINALS, GAME 2

JUNE 2, 2013 · BLACKHAWKS 4, KINGS 2

THE FAST AND THE FURIOUS

Hawks Score on Kings Goalie Early and Often

By Tim Sassone

Jonathan Quick had a pretty good seat to watch the last half of Sunday's game at the United Center — from the bench.

The Blackhawks chased arguably the world's best goaltender midway through the second period after scoring their fourth goal on their way to a 4-2 win in Game 2 of the Western Conference finals.

The Hawks lead the best-of-seven series 2-0 heading to Los Angeles for Games 3 and 4.

The Kings are now 1-7 on the road in the playoffs, but they are going home to the Staples Center where they have won 14 postseason games in a row dating back to last season when they won the Stanley Cup.

"I think we expected them to be better than in Game 1 and they were, but we raised our game, too," said Hawks captain Jonathan Toews. "It's going to get tougher and tougher, especially going into their building."

The Kings also trailed St. Louis 2-0 in the first round, losing both games on the road, before rallying to win four in a row.

"They're a good team, and obviously we would have liked to have gotten one or two here," Kings center Jeff Carter said. "But we're going back home and we've played good hockey there."

The Kings appear to have no answer for the Hawks' speed and skill, at least so far in the first two games. Anze Kopitar was a no-show again Sunday with 2 shots while Dustin Brown had just 1 shot on goal.

"We've played our game and matched lines pretty well," Hawks center Andrew Shaw said. "Now going in their barn they might have something different for us. We've just got to stay composed and compete. I think we have confidence now to play the game we need to play."

Quick didn't get much help from his teammates, especially in the second period.

It was already 2-0 when Bryan Bickell got credit for a goal that Kings defenseman Robyn Regehr actually put into his own net on a Hawks power play at 7:11.

Quick was gone after Michal Handzus beat him on a 2-on-1 with Patrick Sharp at 9:20. Handzus looked off Sharp and beat Quick with a hard wrist shot to make it 4-0.

"We went through a little spurt there in the last series where pucks weren't going in, but now we're getting the results we want," Toews said. "I'm sure a guy like (Quick), he's a competitor and he's going to bounce back. We've got to be even

Marcus Kruger is unfazed as L.A.'s Jeff Carter hovers over him in Game 2. (John Starks/Daily Herald)

16
EASTON
16
BAUER
WARRIOR

tougher on him and try our best not to let him get his confidence back."

It was the Hawks' fifth straight win since going down 3-1 to Detroit in the previous round.

"That's hockey," Toews said. "One day things don't look so good, but you battle your way back and the next thing you know you're feeling pretty good. Momentum can swing pretty quick throughout the playoffs. We understand we're feeling good about where we are in the series, but that's not a team that's going to give up to easy. They're going to keep fighting to battle their way back in the series.

"We can't be satisfied or anything. We can't expect that our momentum is just going to carry us through the next couple games. We've got to work to keep that going."

Shaw opened the scoring at 1:56 when he took a behind-the-back pass from Viktor Stalberg and beat Quick with a shot that went off the post and in.

Nick Leddy didn't get an assist but his pinch along the boards knocked the puck loose. It stayed that way until 19:09 of the first when Brent Seabrook beat Quick to the far side from the right circle after taking a drop pass from Marian Hossa.

"I thought we played all right," Kings coach Darryl Sutter said. "We gave them some wide-open opportunities that they scored on. One is a forecheck right away early in the game. We didn't make the play in the wall we could have made. Then the goal at the end of the first was a read play."

Corey Crawford was terrific in the opening 20 minutes with 13 saves. One of them came against Tyler Toffoli after a crazy bounce off the glass sent the puck toward the net. Toffoli was in the lineup in place of Mike Richards, who was a late scratch because of an upper body injury. ■

Brent Seabrook erupts into a spontaneous goal celebration after scoring in the first period of Game 2. (John Starks/Daily Herald)

ver
KINGS
LA
7
26
BAUER

WESTERN CONFERENCE FINALS, GAME 3

JUNE 4, 2013 • KINGS 3, BLACKHAWKS 1

KINGS GRAB MOMENTUM FROM HAWKS

Duncan Keith Receives Controversial High Sticking Penalty

By Tim Sassone

It was a case of too little too late for the Blackhawks on Tuesday night.

The Hawks failed to get their speed game going until the third period and by that time they were chasing the Kings, who got back in the Western Conference finals with a 3-1 victory at Staples Center.

The momentum now sides with the Kings going into Thursday's Game 4 in Los Angeles.

"They've got the momentum back in the series," Hawks captain Jonathan Toews said. "We didn't want to give that to them, but they played a good game and we didn't have enough to get the result we wanted.

"We still like where we are in the series, but we know we definitely have to bounce back and have a much better effort in Game 4."

The Hawks had only 10 shots in the first two periods before putting 10 on Jonathan Quick in the third period.

"We knew they were going to play well in their building, and they did," Patrick Sharp said. "It's time to regroup and be better next game. We've got to find a way to not only generate more shots but better quality shots."

The game was not without its controversy. Kings coach Darryl Sutter was unhappy with the four-minute minor penalty Duncan Keith received in the second period for high sticking Jeff Carter in the face well behind the play.

Sutter felt the penalty should have been more severe, and replays backed him up. Keith took a two-handed swipe at Carter.

"I didn't think it was a four-minute penalty," Sutter said. "That was the wrong call. It was retaliation."

Keith said it was an accident.

"I wanted to give him a tap, but not where I got him," Keith said. "I'm glad to see that he came back. It was just a little scuffle at the end of the play. It was an accident."

Keith was asked if he was concerned the league might review the play.

"I don't know," he said. "I have no idea. I just said it was an accident."

The Kings played again without No. 2 center Mike Richards, who suffered a concussion in Game 1 when Dave Bolland hit him in the last two minutes. It didn't matter.

Tyler Toffoli, Richards' replacement on a line centered by Carter, picked up an assist in the second period on Slava Voynov's goal to give him a goal and 2 assists in the last two games.

Toffoli is a pretty valuable guy to be able to plug into the lineup if you're Sutter.

"He scored 50-some goals his last year, 19 goals in the minors, rookie of the year in the American League," Sutter said. "Played 60-some games. We brought him up when we had the roster spot to do it, not so much to play him, but because we thought he was close so he could watch and sort of progress is all it is."

It was a strong bounce-back game for Quick, although he faced only 20 shots. "We need great goaltending to beat Chicago," Sutter said.

The Kings got the all-important first goal at 3:21 when Justin Williams took a pass from Voynov and beat Corey Crawford to the short side from inside the left circle.

The goal resulted from a Nick Leddy turnover along the boards.

Voynov's goal came at 6:37 of the second period on somewhat of a broken play that finished with a broken stick. Toffoli had the puck roll off his stick right to Voynov, who was cutting to the net from the right side, and he broke his stick on the shot that beat Crawford.

"Obviously that's a good break," Toffoli said. "I think a couple of guys were in front, and Crawford didn't see it. Any goal is a good goal in the playoffs."

Bryan Bickell scored his seventh goal of the playoffs with 33.6 seconds left in the second period on a wraparound through Quick.

The Hawks pressed for the tying goal in the third period but couldn't get it. Quick robbed Bickell with three minutes left. Dwight King added an empty netter.

"In the third I thought we came at him, came to the net with traffic and got opportunities," Bickell said. "Being up 2-0 on these guys, you saw what they did against St. Louis. They're a great home ice team."

The Kings are 8-0 at the Staples Center, where they have won 15 straight over the last two seasons.

"Their work ethic and their speed and their physical play led to everything else," Toews said. "We didn't quite match it. As a team we have more energy and more speed than we showed tonight." ■

Brandon Saad maintains control of the puck after losing his footing against L.A.'s Anze Kopitar in the first period of Game 3. (AP Images)

WESTERN CONFERENCE FINALS, GAME 4

JUNE 6, 2013 • BLACKHAWKS 3, KINGS 2

HOLLYWOOD ENDING

Hossa's Goal Puts Blackhawks Closer to Stanley Cup Finals

By Tim Sassone

Give Blackhawks coach Joel Quenneville at least part of the credit for Thursday's 3-2 win over the Kings at the Staples Center.

It was Quenneville who tweaked his top two lines late in the second period, and it paid off in goals by Patrick Kane and Marian Hossa to rally the Hawks from a 2-1 deficit.

Kane was bumped up to play with Jonathan Toews and Bryan Bickell and scored his first goal of the series late in the second period at 18:21 to tie it.

Hossa was dropped to the second line with Michal Handzus and Patrick Sharp and responded with the winning goal at 1:10 of the third period on a 2-on-1 with Handzus.

"Just give them a different look," Bickell said. "Great call by Q because it worked and we're happy to get the win."

Quenneville said he was looking for some sort of spark.

"We were behind and I still didn't mind how we were playing at that point in the game," Quenneville said. "Sometimes you get one, and we did. Scoring early in the third really helped us."

The Hawks played without defenseman Duncan Keith, but it was hard to tell. The Kings had just 2 shots in the third period and were 0-for-3 on the power play.

Brent Seabrook, Niklas Hjalmarsson, Michal Rozsival and Johnny Oduya responded with monster games, picking up the bulk of Keith's minutes.

"They did a good job of plugging it off and defending the lead," Kings coach Darryl Sutter said. "The reason they're a great defensive team, and they've been all year, is not just with their goaltender but the way they spread their minutes out.

"Basically what happens is you take that guy out of their lineup and it gives four other top guys a few more minutes. It doesn't really hurt them at all, to be quite honest."

Hjalmarsson had 2 assists and was plus-2 in almost 25 minutes. Seabrook played a game-high 26:20 and had 3 blocked shots and 3 hits. Rozsival played more than 25 minutes and took 32 shifts, 1 fewer than Seabrook.

"I'm just glad I was able to step in there and do a good job," Rozsival said. "I never feel tired after a win. After a loss, I feel tired."

The Hawks lead the Western Conference finals 3-1.

"We need to just play well defensively," Hossa said. "When we play a checking game we are a much better team. The fourth game is always the toughest when you're trying to close it."

Patrick Kane soars over Jonathan Quick after scoring a goal in the second period of Game 4. (AP Images)

KANE
88
WARRIOR
VAUGHN

Kane's goal came a day after he sat at his locker and was highly critical of himself about his lack of production. You just knew he was going to have a big game.

"Kaner wanted the puck, had it early and had it a lot," Quenneville said. "He was dangerous off the rush and took some shots through the screens. It was nice to see him score as well."

Kane was determined to make a difference.

"I think the biggest thing was just trying to get the puck any way I could, skate with it, feel into the game, no matter how that was," Kane said. "I thought I did a good job of that."

The Hawks and Kings were tied at 1-1 after the first period with Slava Voynov and Bickell trading goals.

Bickell's goal came at 13:16 and was a gift as Kings goalie Jonathan Quick muffed a wrist shot from between the circles. It was Bickell's eighth goal of the playoffs, trickling into the net off Quick's glove.

Corey Crawford gave the goal right back early in the second period when he pushed a soft rebound to Dustin Penner in front of the net. But in fairness to Crawford, Nick Leddy got beat to the net and Sheldon Brookbank lost Penner in front.

Hjalmarsson wore the alternate captain's "A" for Keith and also played with Seabrook. Rozsival skated with Oduya as Quenneville basically went with four defensemen.

The Hawks' depth was tested for one of the rare times this season.

"We didn't have to go through any adversity through the season and we've been pretty healthy," Rozsival said.

The Hawks missed Keith during a 5-on-3 power play in the second period that lasted 53 seconds. With Leddy in Keith's spot at the left point, the Hawks were never a threat to score and finished with no shots. Leddy spent most of the time looking to set up Hossa to shoot.

The loss was the first of the playoffs at home for the Kings, who had their 15-game winning streak at Staples Center snapped as well.

"It was a huge win, especially the way they're playing at home," Kane said. "I think they won 15 in a row here at the Staples Center, so it was nice to come in and steal one for sure.

"We put ourselves in a good spot, but by no means do we feel the series is over." ■

Michael Frolik moves the puck to the middle of the ice as Jake Muzzin tries to cut him off in the first period. (AP Images)

67
CCM
67
Reebok
Reebok

WESTERN CONFERENCE FINALS, **GAME 5**

JUNE 8, 2013 • BLACKHAWKS 4, KINGS 3 (2OT)

KINGS DETHRONED

Kane's Goal Lifts Hawks to Dramatic Victory

By Tim Sassone

The last time Patrick Kane scored a hat trick in a clinching game he made Vancouver's Roberto Luongo cry.

There were no tears from Kings goalie Jonathan Quick on Saturday night, only frustration as Kane's third goal at 11:40 of double overtime sailed past his glove and gave the Hawks a 4-3 win.

The dramatic victory at the United Center sends the Hawks back to the Stanley Cup Finals for the second time in four years to play the Boston Bruins. It's going to be the first meeting of Original Six teams for the Cup in 34 years.

Kane beat Quick from inside the right circle on a 2-on-1 with Jonathan Toews for his second career playoff hat trick. His first came in Game 6 against Luongo and the Canucks on May 11, 2009.

"Right now I think it's almost like I'm in a different zone, like in the twilight zone or something," Kane said. "I'm kind of out of it. It's definitely a good feeling."

Kane snapped off a shot into an open net for his fourth goal in the last two games.

"It was certainly an outstanding game by him," Hawks coach Joel Quenneville said. "A great play on the winning goal by Johnny. I thought Kaner played a heck of a game in Games 4 and 5 for us. He stepped up. He took on the responsibility of leading the team. He proved he's a top player in the game."

Even Kings coach Darryl Sutter agreed it was a great play by two of the game's biggest stars.

"In the end, probably their two best offensive guys made a great play to score a goal," Sutter said.

"He's an awesome player," Hawks goalie Corey Crawford said of Kane. "Obviously, I don't know what to say right now. That was awesome.

"I've dreamed about (going to the Finals) my whole life. It's nice, man. It's nice to finally get there after all the work, but there's still a lot to do."

The Hawks failed to hold an early 2-0 lead, as well as a 3-2 with less than a minute to play, with the Kings getting a goal from Mike Richards with 9.4 seconds left in regulation to force overtime.

"Man, nine seconds left and they score," Crawford said.

"We've been there before and you just keep playing," Patrick Sharp said. "It's playoff hockey. No lead is safe. You can't really change the way

Patrick Kane adds to his clutch goal-scoring legend, tying the game with less than four minutes left in regulation in Game 5. (John Starks/Daily Herald)

THE PRIVATEBANK
DISC
COLD AS THE ROCKIES
88
BAUER
KINGS
LA

you play. It's a tough situation emotionally, giving up that goal, but you keep playing hockey."

The Kings finished the postseason 1-8 on the road, losing their last six straight.

"We just didn't have it against these guys," Kings center Jarret Stoll said. "We just couldn't find a way to win a road game."

The Hawks jumped out to a 2-0 lead less than six minutes into the first period on goals by Duncan Keith and Kane.

Sutter called both goals soft.

The Hawks looked like they were going to win and advance to the Finals when Kane scored his second goal of the night with 3:52 to play in the third period, taking a pass from Bickell behind the net and beating Quick.

But the Kings had other ideas. With Quick pulled for a sixth attacker, Richards tied the game on a tip-in from in front after Toews lost a faceoff to Stoll following a disastrous icing against Bickell.

Richards won the draw and headed to the net to deflect a shot by Anze Kopitar past Crawford.

Now it's the Bruins who come to town ready to try to beat the Hawks.

"I've been watching Boston play in the East — they look like they're rolling," Sharp said. "Another tough series ahead of us, but it's an exciting time.

"I really don't know what to expect. It's going to be fun to play against a team that we haven't seen all year. Our scouts and coaches will prepare us, but until you get out and play against those guys, you don't really know what to expect." ■

Corey Crawford shovels the puck away from the net in Game 5. (John Starks/Daily Herald)

Reebok
Reebok
Reebok
Reebok
26
26

John Starks/Daily Herald